TERROR AND
URBAN GUERRILLAS

BOOKS BY JAY MALLIN

Fortress Cuba
Caribbean Crisis
Terror in Viet Nam

Series on Unconventional Warfare

"Che" Guevara on Revolution
Strategy for Conquest
Terror and Urban Guerrillas

TERROR
AND
URBAN
GUERRILLAS

A Study of Tactics and Documents

Edited and with an Introduction by
JAY MALLIN

UNIVERSITY OF MIAMI PRESS
Coral Gables, Florida

To all victims of terror

<u>*NOTICE.*</u>

Here hangs Private Samuel Jones, of Co; B 5th Ohio Regt; by order of Major Genl. Pickett, in retaliation for Private Daniel Bright, of Co; L, 62nd Georgia Regt, (Col Griffins) hung Dec: 18th 1863, by Order of Brig: Genl; Wild..

(*U.S. Civil War, 1863*)

CONTENTS

PREFACE

For the first time in its history the United States is faced with the problem of terroristic activities on the domestic scene. In Viet Nam, the United States is involved in assisting the South Vietnamese to suppress the terroristic activities of the Viet Cong. In Latin America, American diplomats are a target of revolutionary assassins and kidnappers.

This volume is aimed at setting forth the theory and techniques of terror, as described by its leading proponents and practitioners. If we fully understand the methods of and reasons for terrorism, we will be in a far better position to eliminate it. To that end these basic documents have been compiled, together with explanatory material derived from library research as well as my firsthand witness to terrorism in Cuba and South Viet Nam.

For his assistance and encouragement, my gratitude goes to Lt. Col. Peter Kosutic, chief of the counterinsurgency section of the U.S. Air Force's Special Operations School. The school, at which I have been privileged to be a guest lecturer, does outstanding work in acquainting American as well as allied military personnel with the problems of unconventional warfare. In bringing together civilian and military experts from around the country, the school enables them to engage in fruitful exchanges of ideas. My thanks also to Paul A. Jureidini, of the Center for Research in Social Systems, for reading a portion of the manuscript and making useful suggestions, and to Stephen T. Hosmer, of the Rand Corporation, for his assistance in obtaining material related to Viet Nam.

J. M.

TERROR AND
URBAN GUERRILLAS

INTRODUCTION

Human violence—violence committed on humans by humans—today occupies a wide spectrum of real and potential activities. A barroom brawl is violence; so is nuclear warfare.

Terror tactics occupy a portion of the overall spectrum. Obviously the threat of a nuclear war—or the threat of a physical beating to an individual—can be viewed as forms of terror; but these lie within the broad, semantic meaning of the word. In the context of internal political struggle, terror has two basic applications. Dictatorial regimes often maintain themselves in power through the use of terror tactics. These tactics characteristically include arbitrary arrests, tortures, murders, kangaroo courts, lengthy imprisonments, and close vigilance over the words, thoughts, and activities of citizens. This is one side of the coin. The other side is the commission by revolutionary organizations of acts of violence whose psychological effects are expected to further the causes pursued by those groups, the desired end result almost invariably being the overthrow of the existing government. This study will confine itself to the second application of terrorism: the struggle for power.[1]

The basis of terror tactics is the threat—threat to a government that it must abandon power or face continued trouble and danger for its officials; threat to a population that they face constant disruption unless they help overthrow the government. A village chief is assassinated and the threat of death discourages capable men from assuming the local leadership. A diplomat or an airliner is seized, and as a result political prisoners are released because of the threat to the lives of the hostages. The cave man is still swinging his rock. . . .

Terrorism is a form of guerrilla warfare. The basic tactic for guerrilla warfare is to hit and run and hide, hit, run, hide. Guerrillas conceal themselves in mountainous or rural areas. Terror tactics are employed in urban areas as well. When carried out in cities and towns, they are often aptly referred to as "urban guerrilla warfare." Like guerrilla warfare, terrorism is a hit, run, and hide form of conflict—combat by attrition, with the destruction of the prevailing authority being the hoped-for end result. Often, although not always, guerrilla warfare and urban clandestine activities are conducted simultaneously and are complementary to each other. Such was the case in Cuba in 1957-58, in Venezuela in the early sixties, and in Viet Nam for over two decades.

Terror tactics are not a new weapon. One of the most famous acts of terrorism of this century was committed in the then-Austrian town of Sarajevo on 28 June 1914: a double assassination of royalty which precipitated World War I. Abraham Lincoln was the victim of a terror plot hatched by a small group of Southern sympathizers who hoped to destroy the Union government. Fidel Castro was still a child in short pants at a time Cuba was immersed in a bloody clandestine struggle aimed at overthrowing the dictator of that period.

The complex, crowded, interrelated modern world appears to be exceptionally vulnerable to political terror tactics. Electronic communications bind the various countries and peoples closely together. When Archduke Francis Ferdinand and his wife were assassinated in Sarajevo, the news reached Germany's Kaiser Wilhelm via an admiral on a launch who placed a piece of paper in a cigarette case and tossed it aboard Wilhelm's yacht. President Richard Nixon was flying aboard the presidential plane in the United States in September 1970 when a radio message crackled in to inform him that an American airliner had been blown up in far-off Cairo, Egypt, after having been hijacked.

Today's communications systems provide a long tunnel along which the reverberations of a terrorist act can travel far and fast. A diplomat is kidnapped in one country and within minutes the foreign ministry of his own country receives the news and brings pressures to bear in an effort to secure his release. Raisuli, a Moroccan bandit, in May of 1904 kidnapped Ion Perdicaris, believed to be an American citizen. It was a month, however, before Theodore Roosevelt issued, through his secretary of state, his famous ultimatum, "Perdicaris alive or Raisuli dead."[2]

Delicately balanced international relationships are susceptible to acts of terror. Two bullets at Sarajevo shattered the peace of the world for four years. Airplane hijackings by Palestinian terrorists in September 1970 endangered a Mid East ceasefire which had been carefully worked out to prevent an eventual confrontation between the two superpowers, the United States and the Soviet Union.

Delicately constructed equipment is also highly vulnerable to acts of terror. A hammer can destroy a computer. A match can level an industrial plant. Within the space of a few weeks in 1970 the huge airliner in Cairo and a highly sophisticated research center in Madison, Wisconsin, were blown up by explosives placed by terrorists. One or two men can pulverize the accumulated work and knowledge of many men. It is easier to destroy than to build, and, tragically, as man builds ever more complicated equipment, the gap between simple ability to destroy and complexity of construction grows wider; and it is into this gap that the terrorist has moved. Once largely limited to killing people, the terrorist today has the whole, wide field of technological development as his potential hunting ground. In order to further a cause, one no longer needs an army, or at least a guerrilla group; a fuse or a hammer will now suffice. Fill a harmless Coca-Cola bottle with gasoline obtained at a filling station, attach a wick, and you have a deadly, destructive Molotov cocktail. With this a person can bring down a telephone pole, destroy electrical circuitry, or hijack an airliner.

Terror tactics usually encompass three basic types of activity: killings, bombings, and kidnappings (including hijackings, which are a form of mass kidnapping). Ordinarily all three methods are employed when a clandestine movement launches a terror campaign. Acts of sabotage can have, but not always necessarily do have, terroristic goals. Sabotage will add to the intensity of a terror campaign, but in general it aims at the destruction of material objectives, the primary purpose being to inflict damage on the economy of the land.

In considering types of action, it must not be overlooked that sometimes more than one factor—not only the terror purpose—is involved in a deed or series of deeds. The murder of village leaders may be the policy of a clandestine group; the person carrying out an actual killing may be acting out of personal revenge. The hijacking of airliners may be the policy of another group; an individual hijacker may be acting as much in search of "glory" as because of superior orders.

It must also be noted that an act of violence may serve more than one purpose. When a village official is murdered, authority is destroyed and at the same time a terror effect is engendered which is felt throughout the village's population and particularly among other officials and governmental adherents.

Variations in patterns of terror appear in different countries. These variations are determined by local circumstances, as:

In Guatemala in 1968, with both rightist and leftist elements engaged in terroristic activities, revenge killings were a characteristic of the violence. In addition, kidnappings for ransom became almost commonplace as terrorists favored this method for obtaining funds.

In Uruguay in the late sixties, the Tupamaros, an extremist organization, first cultivated a Robin Hood image by such deeds as robbing a casino. This image, evoking laughter more than concern within the populace, enabled the Tupamaros to establish themselves as an operational and well-known organization. They then turned to more deadly activities, including the murder of a kidnapped American official.

In eastern India, Maoist youths known as Naxalites carried out a campaign of terror in 1940. Believing in violence as the means to destroy the established order, they were responsible for killings and bombings, with bomb explosions sometimes occurring at the rate of two a day. Naxalites seized lands in rural areas, which resulted in armed conflicts with landowners.

Terror in Viet Nam in the late fifties was largely selective (i.e., the killing of village chiefs). Later it was expanded to include general targets (i.e., a mine placed in a road to catch any passing vehicle). The wider scope was given to terrorism as the Viet Cong increased their efforts to bring down the South Vietnamese government.

The Cuban revolution of the late fifties was a classic case of a clandestine struggle linked with guerrilla combat. Fidel Castro led the rebel guerrillas and became the romantic symbol of the revolution. In the cities and towns, however, the underground also waged its battle against the government. Significantly, more rebels died in the cities than in the hills. The underground engaged in numerous terrorist activities, with varying degrees of success. There were some assassination attempts (few succeeded) and a good many acts of sabotage.

The explosion of bombs was, however, the most potent weapon utilized by the Cuban underground. Bombs exploded in stores, theatres, and night clubs and on the streets. The bombs served several purposes: loud blasts demonstrated to one and all, friend and foe, that the rebel underground existed and was highly active. The bombs encouraged the population, which was largely anti-government, and helped to demoralize the regime's forces, which were aware that the enemy was present and dangerous. In May of 1957 a mighty explosion destroyed a section of a vital electrical conduit in Havana, and part of the city was blacked out for more than two days. In November of the same year residents of Havana thought they had come under bombardment when some forty bombs exploded in different places within a fifteen-minute period. As these and other terrorist acts were carried out, commerce slowed, investment capital dried up, tourism came to a halt, and the decline in the economy became a major factor in eventually bringing down the government.

A question which terrorists everywhere have confronted is: Does terrorism in the long run do more harm than good, turning a population against the cause espoused by the terrorists? The Cuban underground, operating within a population that was basically sympathetic, sought to solve this problem by not using, in at least some cases, any metal in its bombs. This minimized casualties because flying metal fragments do the most harm to humans, not the explosions themselves, if the latter are limited in potency. The bombs were exploded primarily for their psychological effects, not to kill or maim. There were some casualties, but these were relatively few when compared to the large numbers of civilians killed or wounded by Viet Cong explosions, whose primary purpose is precisely to kill and wound.

The Cuban revolution was the incubator for two terror methods that have now come into international use: hijackings of aircraft and kidnapping of people for political purposes.[3] The rebel 26 of July Movement was probably the first organization to carry out hijackings for political reasons. A number of domestic flights and one international flight were seized by hijackers, who thus sought to disrupt the country's communications system and to demonstrate the ability of the rebels to strike appreciable blows.

In February of 1958 Juan Manuel Fangio, the then auto racing world champion, was in Havana to participate in a race that was to be held in that city. Members of the rebel underground seized Fangio in the lobby of a downtown hotel, spirited him off, and held him for several days, finally releasing him unharmed. No demands were made: the kidnapping in itself served the rebels' purpose. The daring act brought them worldwide publicity as well as demonstrated the rebels' capability for action within a city which was thought of as a government stronghold.

Four months later the rebels staged an even more spectacular kidnapping. Guerrillas led by Raúl Castro had occupied a portion of easternmost Cuba, but there they were being harassed by the government's aircraft. In an effort to obtain a breathing spell, the rebels seized forty-eight Americans and two Canadians. The rebels knew the government was unlikely to bomb guerrilla-held areas as long as American citizens might be endangered. By means of this mass kidnapping the rebels achieved a number of objectives: they demonstrated their effective control of a portion of the national territory; they forced a letup in the government's air activity; and they won de facto recognition of sorts from the United States when two American consuls came to negotiate the release of the prisoners.

The hijackings and kidnappings by the Cuban rebels were an ominous portent of the future use of these techniques by terrorist groups in other parts of the world. The hijacking of airliners reached a climax early in September 1970 when nine Palestinian terrorists seized four airliners, carrying 578 passengers and crewmen, within a period of four days. (A fifth hijacking attempt was thwarted.) All four of the seized planes were subsequently blown up.

With the failure of a number of castroite guerrilla movements in Latin America during the sixties, revolutionaries began concentrating their efforts on urban warfare. A novel technique that was developed was the kidnapping of foreign diplomats. The diplomats would be held and demands issued by the terrorists that certain political prisoners be released. Faced with the embarrassment of having diplomats accredited to them being held by revolutionary groups, several governments acceded to the demands and released the prisoners, permitting them to fly to other countries. In some cases governments refused to give in, and as a result several diplomats were murdered. In the period 1968-70 eleven diplomats were kidnapped.[4] Two of these were murdered. In addition, a U.S. ambassador (John Gordon Mein in Guatemala) was killed when he attempted to flee from would-be kidnappers. (In Canada also two officials were seized by terrorists, and one of these was killed.)

Nowhere in the world in modern times has terror been used so extensively as a political weapon as the Communists have employed it in South Viet Nam. The terror tactic has ranked with the military tactic as a full-fledged component of the Communist drive to conquer that country. The Communist military commander, General Vo Nguyen Giap, stated bluntly:

> At the price of their hard-won experiences, our compatriots in the South realized that the fundamental trend of imperialism and its lackeys is violence and war; that is why *the most correct path to be followed by the peoples to liberate themselves is revolutionary violence and revolutionary war*. [Italics are Giap's.] This path conforms strictly to the ethics and the fundamentals of Marxism-Leninism on class struggle, on the state and the revolution. Only by revolutionary violence can the masses defeat aggressive imperialism and its lackeys and overthrow the reactionary administration to take power.[5]

So pervasive has terrorism become that one writer asserted that this "has long passed the stage of excess and become a vice, an intoxication with violence, one that may well be a release from the terrible and inhumanly prolonged hardships and repressions of personal interests which its adherents must undergo."[6]

Terrorism may well be an emotional outlet for persons engaging in it. It has, however, also served very real political purposes for the Communists in Viet Nam. A study of Viet Cong terror tactics by the U.S. Mission in Viet Nam enumerated five aims the Communists hope to accomplish by employing these methods. The five goals are:

1. *Morale building within the Viet Cong ranks.* A successful terrorist act does much to create an aura of invulnerability within a guerrilla band and helps bolster spirits throughout the insurgent organization. . . .
2. *Advertising the Viet Cong movement.* . . .
3. *Disorientation and psychological isolation of the individual.* This is done by destroying the structure of authority which previously was a source of security. The particular target is the Vietnamese villager. . . . Terror removes the underpinnings of the orderly system in which the villager lives out his life. . . .
4. *Elimination of opposing forces.* . . . By means of terror the Viet Cong have sought to eliminate the entire leader class of Vietnamese villagers. . . .
5. *Provocation of the GVN* [Government of South Viet Nam]. . . . Any government faced with terrorism must attempt to suppress the terrorists. Ideally, that suppression is by an orthodox use of law enforcement. But if the terrorist is effective and if the government sees itself in a crisis, it will almost inevitably use extraordinary repressive measures.[7]

As previously noted, the Communists have utilized both selective and general methods of terror in Viet Nam. A selective target may be a village chief, a policeman or an American official. A general target may be an audience in a theatre or people crowding into a market place. In hitting a specific target, the terrorist strikes at the fabric of governmental control. In hitting a general target, he aims at the overall social fabric. Create chaos, the terrorist believes, and open the way to seizing power.

The widespread Communist use of terror in Viet Nam since 1957 has been documented in a considerable number of publications. Statistics related to events in Viet Nam are often suspect, but they can serve as indicatory guides. According to available information, assassinations in 1961 totalled 500, rose to 3,707 in 1967, and then to 6,338 in 1968. (The 1968 figure is not considered complete due to the impossibility of counting all the dead at the time of the bloody Tet offensive.) In 1969 and 1970, with United States and South Vietnamese forces in more effective control, assassinations dropped somewhat. The following chart provides some idea of the extent of Communist terrorism during the period 1961-1970:[8]

VIET CONG TERRORISM STATISTICS

	1961[a]	1962[d]	1963[d]	1964[e]	1965[e]	1966[f]	1967[gc]	1968[hi]	1969[h]	1970[h]
Assassinated	500	1,719	2,073	1,795	1,900	1,732	3,707	6,338	6,090	5,951
Wounded	[b]	6,458	8,375	2,131	1,467	[b]	8,072	15,918	15,063	12,588
Abducted	1,000	9,688	7,262	9,554	7,992	3,810	5,357	10,108	6,097	6,872
Incidents[c]							4,155	11,931	10,526	11,680

[a] Source: *A Threat to the Peace* (U.S. Department of State, 1961). These figures cover only the first six months of 1961.

[b] No figures available.

[c] Incidents not compiled until May 1967.

[d] Source: South Vietnamese Government report to the International Control Commission.

[e] Source: Defense Intelligence Agency, based on U.S. Mission reports.

[f] Source: Public Safety Directorate, Civil Operations and Rural Development Support.

[g] Source: National Police.

[h] Source: National Police and Combined Intelligence Center, Viet Nam.

[i] Figures for 1968 are not considered complete due to the confusion caused by the Communists' Tet offensive.

The Communists launched an attack in 1968 which enabled them to occupy most of Hue, the country's second city. Later, once the city had been recaptured by government and American forces, it was discovered that the Communists had massacred a large number of people. The mass graves of the victims were found around the city. Douglas Pike has provided this description:

> The first discovery of communist victims came in the Gia Hoi High School yard, on February 26; eventually 170 bodies were recovered. In the next few months 18 additional grave sites were found, the largest of which were Tang Quang Tu Pagoda (67 victims), Bai Dau (77), Cho Thong area (an estimated 100), the imperial tombs area (201), Thien Ham (approximately 200), and Dong Gi (approximately 100). In all almost 1,200 bodies were found in hastily dug, poorly concealed graves. At least half of these showed clear evidence of atrocity killings: hands wired behind backs, rags stuffed in mouths, bodies contorted but without wounds (indicating burial alive). The other nearly 600 bore wound marks but there was no way of determining whether they died by firing squad or incidental to the battle. Among these victims were three West German doctors, a medical technician who was the wife of one of the doctors, and two French Catholic priests, one of whom was buried alive.[9]

More graves were subsequently uncovered. Some 2,800 bodies were found in the various graves, and in addition close to 2,000 persons were missing.

Pike has categorized by phases the changing Communist rationale behind the killings:

First days	We are to be here for a short while only.	Eliminate "enemies of the revolution," weaken the structure of the establishment.
Middle period	We are here to stay.	Purge the old social order, liquidate "social negatives."
Final period	We are going to be driven out.	Liquidate anyone in Communist hands who can identify individual party members.[10]

General Giap has stated, as previously quoted, that "violence and war" conform "to the ethics and the fundamentals of Marxism-Leninism." Communists openly favor the use of violence and terror as a means to obtain political control; rarely do they attempt to conceal their adherence to, often preference of, the utilization of force. The Communist Manifesto states bluntly: "They [the Communists] openly declare that their ends can be attained only by the forcible overthrow of all existing social conditions."[11] Karl Marx wrote in *Das Kapital*, "Force is the midwife of every old society pregnant with a new one,"[12] and almost a century later Ernesto Guevara echoed Marx with the statement, ". . . We should not fear violence, the midwife of new societies . . ."[13] China's Mao Tse-tung clearly set forth the Communist viewpoint on violence when he said, "Every Communist must grasp the truth, 'Political power grows out of the barrel of a gun.' "[14]

Terrorist campaigns follow a pattern. At first there are sporadic activities, without much design. Usually these consist of occasional and scattered bombings, and perhaps one or two assassination attempts. These actions are similar to the first tentative attacks that are carried out by a guerrilla group beginning operations in a rural area. If the army is unable to snuff out the guerrilla movement, it expands and becomes more active and dangerous. In urban areas, if a clandestine terrorist apparatus is not eliminated completely, it, too, may grow and become more sophisticated.

One indication of sophistication is the ability of a terror group to select and carry out attacks on specific targets. This frequently takes the form of attacks on police. Lenin once wrote, "The first objective [of armed struggle] is to kill individuals such as high officials and lower-ranking members of the police and army."[15] The politically-motivated killing of policemen dates back at least to the first decade of this century, when it was employed as a tactic by revolutionaries fighting against the czarist government of Russia. Leon Trotsky has provided an account:

> In the Caucasus, with its romantic traditions of highway robbery and gory feuds still very much alive, guerrilla warfare found any number of fearless practitioners. More than a thousand terrorist acts of all kinds were perpetrated in Transcaucasia alone during 1905-1907, the years of the First Revolution. Fighting detachments found also a great spread of activity in the Urals, under the leadership of the Bolsheviks, and in Poland under the banner of the P.P.S. (Polish Socialist Party). On the second of August, 1906, scores of policemen and soldiers were assassinated on the streets of Warsaw and other Polish cities. According to the explanation of the leaders, the purpose of these attacks was "to bolster the revolutionary mood of the proletariat."[16]

In recent times revolutionary groups have continued the practice of murdering police officers. In South Viet Nam the police have been a primary target of Viet Cong terrorists. Not only have individual policemen been shot but even police headquarters have been attacked. In the Dominican Republic, at the time of the 1965 uprising, so many police were attacked and killed by terrorists in Santo Domingo, the capital city, that the police disappeared from the streets of the city. Police are a symbol of the existing order; they are also a major support of that order. To strike at the police is to deal psychological as well as real blows against the existing establishment.

In the United States, today troubled by terrorism for the first time in its history, terror tactics have reached the level of sophistication in which terrorists are leveling their guns at policemen with deadly effect. As of mid-September 1970 sixteen police officers were killed in that year as the result of unprovoked attacks, more than double the total for the previous year and nearly four times the annual average for the past ten years.[17]

There are no simple, ready solutions to terrorist activities; there is no panacea to terrorism. Counterterror is not the answer. It is, in fact, counterproductive. Although limited gains may temporarily be achieved —such as deterring faint-hearted individuals from joining a rebel group —in the long run counterterror will cause repugnance in a population, turning many persons against the authorities. Such was the case in Cuba in 1957 and 1958.

There are, however, techniques that have been applied, sometimes quite successfully, to particular aspects of terrorism. Cuba, during the aforementioned period, eliminated the problem of hijacking by requiring body searches of all passengers and by placing armed, uniformed guards aboard planes. The guards were seated with the crews so that they could keep watchful eyes on the passengers through peepholes set in doors which separated the crew and passenger compartments. Modern electronic equipment is today an additional aid in detecting weapons and forestalling hijackings.

Good police techniques are the best method to beat terrorism, which is, after all, a form—a political variation—of crime. Infiltration of terrorist groups, money payments to informers—the same methods utilized against criminal gangs—are feasible against terror groups. A detailed file, kept up to date—computerized, if this is possible—of all persons suspect of being engaged in clandestine activities can be most helpful, just as files of criminals aid police in crime detection. In one case in a Latin American city files on possible terrorists were combed and over thirty suspects were brought in for interrogation. Of the persons questioned, only one was found to be engaged in terrorist activities; but when he told the authorities what he knew, they were able to break up a significant portion of an underground network.

Terrorist groups must obtain weapons and explosives in order to carry out their work. Strict controls over the sale and distribution of these can make the tasks of terrorists more difficult, and sometimes can enable police to trace the purchases of weapons utilized in acts of terror.

As mentioned, police officers are often the targets of terrorists. By being cautious in situations that are potentially dangerous, police can reduce their risks. Policemen working in pairs are more difficult targets to attack: terrorists must either kill both policemen or chance being killed themselves. If two policemen keep a distance between themselves, when they approach or are approached by a questionable individual, that individual, if he is a terrorist, will find it almost impossible to kill both officers at the same moment.

Security at public buildings, including theatres, can be enhanced if all packages, including women's purses, are subjected to scrutiny at entrances. A stick of dynamite can, of course, be smuggled in under a person's clothing, and it may not be feasible to search every individual fully. Searches of packages and purses, however, will at least decrease the possibility of bombs being smuggled into a building, and certainly eliminate the possibility of any sizeable explosive artifact being introduced into the edifice.

The cities of South Viet Nam have long been troubled by terror campaigns. In order to lessen the casualties and damage inflicted by terrorists, a number of steps have been taken by the authorities. These tactics have included:

Government agents infiltrate the Viet Cong clandestine apparatus. This is one of the most effective methods of keeping track of terrorist activities, sometimes forestalling these before they can be carried out. Agents who have penetrated an underground system can not only identify individual terrorists but often can provide enough information to enable the authorities to destroy an entire clandestine cell or series of cells.

At roads leading into a city, authorities search vehicles to make sure none are carrying weapons or explosives. Within the city itself, police spot-check passing cars (perhaps every fifth or tenth vehicle).

Censuses are conducted frequently in order to keep track of inhabitants. An unexplained "cousin" who has come from the interior might be a Viet Cong agent.

Still another tactic is to cordon off an area within a city suddenly and have the police carefully sweep through that zone. They round up persons who cannot adequately identify themselves or explain their presence.

Secure areas are maintained around or adjoining government buildings. Vehicles entering these areas are subject to search, including by means of a mirrored device that is passed underneath the vehicles to see if explosives have been concealed there.

The military have learned the value of civic action programs which aim at winning over the inhabitants of a troubled area so that they will support the government and its forces and not rebel guerrillas. The same tactic is valid for urban police. If the police do not make an effort at maintaining friendly relations with the inhabitants of a troubled portion of a city, such as a ghetto area, those people are more likely to hide and help terrorists who are striking at the police and the established order. Guerrillas in rural areas need the support of the peasantry. Similarly, urban guerrillas must be assisted by local people if they are to be able to operate effectively and to evade the police.

Urban terror is a cross between crime and insurgency. By adapting the techniques of crime-fighting and counterinsurgency, the best answers to terrorism can be found.

The United States will overcome the problem of terrorism just as it has solved innumerable other difficulties in its 195-year history. The terrorists are an irritation, not a severe danger, within the national fabric. Danger lies in the possibility of change being wrought in the system of justice, not in search of greater justice, but because citizens have lost their trust in the strength of the nation and faith in its ability to overcome its problems.

Set aside justice in the name of law and order, and the country will have neither justice nor true law. The only order then will be that of an imprisoned society. To abandon justice is to assume a moral level hardly better than that of the extremist, the terrorist, the anarchist. A wise American said:

> If there be any among us who would wish to dissolve this Union or to change its republican form, let them stand undisturbed as monuments of the safety with which error of opinion may be tolerated where reason is left free to combat it. I know, indeed, that some honest men fear that a republican government cannot be strong; that this government is not strong enough. But would the honest patriot, in the full tide of successful experiment, abandon a government which has so far kept us free and firm, on the theoretic and visionary fear that this government, the world's best hope, may by possibility want energy to preserve itself? I trust not.[18]

These words were spoken by Thomas Jefferson as part of his first inaugural address, delivered on 4 March 1801.

Coral Gables, 1971

PARTISAN WARFARE 1

by N. Lenin

Hardly a page of Russian history is free of paragraphs written in blood. Pogroms and purges, Ivan the Terrible who slew his son, Joseph Stalin who murdered millions of *kulaks*, cossacks riding, sabres flashing, blood running in the streets, riots and revolutions, assassinations and executions, murder and torture and terror—Mother Russia has suffered all of this. It was in this fertile ground of suffering and turbulence that the ideas of a German journalist named Karl Heinrich Marx took seed. And because the first Marxist government won control through terror and violence, and maintained itself in power through terror and violence, terror and violence have been an integral element of Marxist—Communist—tactics and ideology ever since. On 7 November 1917 the Bolsheviks—later renamed the Communist party—seized control in Russia, and in the years that have followed fifteen nations and one-third of the world's population have fallen to communism.

Until the Chilean presidential election of 1970, not one country had freely chosen the Communist way. Always the Communist conquest had been achieved through the use of military or mob force. Utilizing force to seize power, communism also employed force to retain control. The notorious operations of secret police organizations and the Soviet military crushing of Hungary and Czechoslovakia are stark examples of tactics used by Communists in order to stay in power.

The Social Democratic Labor party was organized in Russia in 1898 and was the leading Marxist movement in that country. In 1903 the party split into two factions: the radical Bolsheviks ("majority") and more moderate Mensheviks ("minority"). The Bolsheviks utilized urban warfare in their efforts to overthrow the czarist government. Their leader, Vladimir Ilyich Ulianov, who adopted and became better known by the name N. Lenin, instructed his followers:

> Go to the youth. Organize at once and everywhere fighting brigades among students, and particularly among workers. Let them arm themselves immediately with whatever weapons they can obtain—rifles, revolvers, bombs, knives, brass knuckles, clubs, rags soaked in kerosene to start fires with, rope or rope ladders, shovels for building barricades, dynamite cartridges, barbed wire, tacks against cavalry. Let the squads begin to train for immediate operations. Some can undertake to assassinate a spy or blow up a police station, others can attack a bank to expropriate funds for an insurrection. Let every squad learn, if only by beating up police.[1]

These orders were given during the revolution of 1905. In January of that year a peaceful demonstration by workers in St. Petersburg was fired on by troops, causing hundreds of deaths. The affair sparked a revolution which lasted until the end of the year, when it was finally suppressed. The rebels turned to terror tactics. A Menshevik leader, Leon Trotsky (he was born Lev Davidovich Bronstein), wrote of this period:

> [The fight of] the routed insurrectionists continued convulsively for a long time in the form of scattered local explosions, guerrilla raids, group and individual terrorist acts. The course of the revolution was characterized with remarkable clarity by statistics of the terror. Two hundred thirty-three persons were assassinated in 1905; 768 in 1906; 1,231 in 1907. The number wounded showed a somewhat different ratio, since the terrorists were learning to be better shots. The terrorist wave reached its crest in 1907. "There were days," wrote a liberal observer, "when several big acts of terror were accompanied by as many as scores of minor attempts and assassinations of lower rank officialdom. . . . Bomb laboratories were established in all cities, the bombs destroying some of their careless makers . . ." and the like.[2]

Terrorism must increase its tempo, at the same time gaining greater popular support for the insurrectional cause, if it is to succeed in its final purpose of overthrowing the established government. In Russia at this time, however, terrorism became a substitute for popular action, and as such was doomed to failure. Trotsky wrote:

> On the whole, the three-year period from 1905 through 1907 is particularly notable for both terrorist acts and strikes. But what stands

out is the divergence between their statistical records: while the number of strikers fell off rapidly from year to year, the number of terrorists acts mounted with equal rapidity. Clearly, individual terrorism increased as the mass movement declined. Yet terrorism could not grow stronger indefinitely. The impetus unleashed by the revolution was bound to spend itself in terrorism as it had spent itself in other spheres. Indeed, while there were 1,231 assassinations in 1907, they dropped to 400 in 1908 and to about a hundred in 1909. The growing percentage of the merely wounded indicated, moreover, that now the shooting was being done by untrained amateurs, mostly by callow youngsters.[3]

A parallel situation has developed in recent times in the United States. Massive disturbances in the sixties did much to awaken the national conscience and brought great strides in the field of civil rights. Once this progress was achieved, obviating the need for further recourse to violence, the extremists who chose to remain extremists resorted to terror tactics. Here again terrorism became a substitute for a popular movement, and as occurred in Russia sixty years ago, political terrorism in the United States will inevitably be suffocated.

The following article by Lenin was published in 1906. Writing against a background of a decade of strikes and uprisings which had failed to unseat the czarist government, Lenin discusses and advocates the utilization of "armed struggle" by the revolutionaries. "Armed struggle" is an euphemism for terrorism, and its aims are set forth bluntly: "The first objective is to kill individuals such as high officials and lower-ranking members of the police and army. The second objective is to confiscate money from the government as well as from private persons."

Lenin does not believe, however, that terrorism alone is sufficient or wise, for this would reduce its practitioners to "the level of drunkards and bums." Terror must be integrated and in harmony with other "methods of combat." In order to be successful, Lenin holds, terrorism must be ideologically guided: "Partisan warfare should be ennobled by the enlightening and organizing influence of socialism." What one fights against, says Lenin, does not count as much as what one fights for. The thesis that tactic and ideology are unitary has remained a constant in the writings of Communist military theoreticians.

PARTISAN WARFARE

The question of partisan actions has aroused great interest within the party and among the workers.[1] We have mentioned this topic repeatedly before. Our present intention is to redeem our promise and summarize our position on this subject.

Let us start from the beginning. What are the basic questions every Marxist must ask when he analyzes the problem of the types of struggle?[2] First of all, unlike primitive forms of socialism, Marxism does not tie the movement to any particular combat method. It recognizes the possibility that struggle may assume the most variegated forms. For that matter, Marxism does not "invent" those forms of struggle. It merely organizes the tactics of strife and renders them suitable for general use. It also renders the revolutionary classes conscious of the forms of the clashes which emerge spontaneously from the activities of the movement. Marxism rejects all abstract thinking and doctrinaire prescriptions about types of struggle. It calls for a careful study of the *mass struggle* which actually is taking place. As the movement develops, as the consciousness of the masses grows, and as the economic and political crises are becoming more intense, ever new and different methods of defense and attack will be used in the conflict. Hence, Marxism never will reject any particular combat method, let alone reject it forever. Marxism does not limit itself to those types of struggle which, at a given moment, are both practical and traditional. It holds that, due to changes in social conditions, new forms of battle will arise *inevitably*, although no one can forsee what the character of these future encounters will be. In this field, if we may say so, Marxism is *learning* from the practice of the masses. It is far from claiming that it should *teach* the masses tactics elaborated in the abstract by strategists of the pen. We know, as Kautsky stated when he was analyzing the different forms of social revolution, that the coming crisis will present us with new and unpredictable forms of action.

Second, Marxism asks that the various types of struggle be analyzed within their *historical* framework. To discuss conflict outside of its historical and concrete setting is to misunderstand elementary dialectic materialism. At various junctures of the economic evolution, and depending upon changing political, national, cultural, social, and other conditions, differing types of struggle may become important and even predominant. As a result of those [sociological] transformations, secondary and subordinate forms of action may change their significance. To try and answer positively or negatively the question of whether a certain tactic is usable, without at the same time studying the concrete conditions confronting a given movement at a precise point of its development, would mean a complete negation of Marxism.

Those are the two basic concepts which must serve as our guide. The soundness of this approach has been confirmed by numerous examples from the history of Western European Marxism. At present, European socialists regard parliamentarism and trade unionism as their main method of struggle. Previously, they favored the armed uprising.[3] Contrary to the opinion of liberal-bourgeois politicians like the Russian Cadets and the Bessaglavtsi,[4] the European socialists are perfectly willing to favor the uprising again should the situation change in the future.

During the 1870s, social democrats rejected the idea that the general strike could be used as a panacea tactic and as a nonpolitical method suitable for the immediate overthrow of the bourgeoisie. But after the experience of 1905,[5] the social democrats fully recognized the political mass strike as *a* means which, under *certain* conditions, could become necessary. Similarly, during the 1840s the social democrats recognized the utility of barricades. By the end of the nineteenth century, conditions had changed and the socialist rejected the barricades as unsuitable. However, after the experience of the Moscow rising, which, in Kautsky's words, demonstrated new tactics of barricade fighting, they were willing to revise their position and again acknowledge the usefulness of barricades.[6]

II

After this exposition of general Marxist doctrine, we want to discuss the Russian revolution. Let us consider the historical development of the various action types to which the revolution gave rise. First, there occurred economic strikes by the workers (1896-1900), then political demonstrations by workers and students (1901-02), peasant unrest (1902), subsequently the beginnings of political mass strikes variously connected with demonstrations (Rostov 1902, strikes during the summer of 1903, the affair of 22 January 1905),[7] political general strike with local barricade fighting (October 1905), mass barricade battles waged by large numbers [of revolutionaries], as well as armed uprising (December 1905), peaceful parliamentary struggle (April-July 1906), local military uprisings (June 1905-June 1906), and local peasant uprisings (fall 1905-fall 1906).

Such was the development of the struggle before the autumn of 1906.

Absolutism opposed these types of struggle with Black Hundreds pogroms.[8] These pogroms were initiated in spring 1903 at Kishinev and ended with the Siedliec pogrom in 1906. During this period, the organizing of Black Hundreds pogroms and the tormenting of Jews, students, revolutionaries and class-conscious workers continued unbated and steadily increased in ferocity. Mob violence was paired with military violence perpetrated by reactionary troops. Artillery was used on villages and cities. Punitive expeditions were dispatched, and all over the railroads there were moving trains crowded with political prisoners.

This, then, has been the general background of the situation. From this background there has emerged the phenomenon of *armed struggle*.[9] Our paper is devoted to the study and evaluation of this new occurrence. Although merely a secondary and incidental part of the whole, armed struggle has been pushed into the foreground. What is armed struggle? What are its forms and its causes? When did it originate? What has been the frequency of its occurrence? What is its significance for the general course of the revolution? What is its connection with the proletarian class struggle organized and waged by social democracy? After having described the general background of the problem, we shall now address ourselves to these questions.

Armed struggle is waged by small groups and individuals, some of whom are members of revolutionary parties. In certain regions of Russia, however, the *majority* [of the partisans] are not affiliated with any revolutionary organization. Armed struggle aims at two *different* objects which must be distinguished *sharply* from one another. The first objective is to kill individuals such as high officials and lower-ranking members of the police and army.[10] The second objective is to confiscate money from the government as well as from private persons. Portions of the captured money are used for party purposes, other portions for arms and the preparation of the rising, and the rest for the sustenance of persons engaging in the struggle described by us.[11] The money seized in the great expropriations (more than 200,000 rubles in the Caucasus and 875,000 rubles in Moscow) was allocated to the revolutionary parties primarily.[12] Smaller expropriations were used mainly, and sometimes exclusively, for the livelihood of the "expropriators." This type of struggle came into widespread use during 1906, after the December uprising [at Moscow]. The aggravation of the political crisis to the point of armed insurrection, and especially the ever growing pauperization, famine, and unemployment in villages and cities, were among the most potent causes leading to the emergence of armed combat. The *declassé* elements of the population, the *Lumpenproletariat* and anarchist groups, chose this struggle as the main and even *only* form of the social war. Autocracy answered with the tactics of martial law, conscription of younger military classes, Black Hundreds pogroms (Siedliec) and court martials.

III

Armed struggle often is considered to be anarchism, Blanquism, old-style terrorism, and, at any rate, an activity perpetrated by isolated individuals out of touch with the masses. The acts of armed struggle are judged to demoralize the workers. Allegedly they divorce broad strata of the population from the toilers, disorganize the revolutionary movement, and hurt the revolutionary cause. Examples supporting this type of evaluation are drawn easily from the daily press.

But how good are these examples? Let us look at one case. Partisan struggle reached its *greatest* popularity in the Lettish districts. On 21 August and 25 September [1906], the newspaper *Novoye Vremya*[13] complained bitterly about the activities of the Lettish socialists. The Lettish Social Democratic party, a branch of the Social Democratic Workers Party of Russia, disclosed a list of police agents. This disclosure was inserted in the party newspaper (circulation: 30,000) and was accompanied by the comment that it was the duty of every honest person to help bring about the liquidation of those spies. The police collaborators were "enemies of the revolution," their property was declared liable to seizure, and they themselves were designated for execution. The social democrats have instructed the population to contribute money to the party, but against stamped receipts only. In the latest budget, there was listed among the party's annual receipts totalling 48,000 rubles an item of 5,600 rubles expropriated by the Libau organization for the purchase of weapons. Of course, *Novoye Vremya* is outraged by such "revolutionary legislation" and by this "terror regime."

No one would dare call those actions by the Lettish social democrats anarchism, Blanquism or terrorism. Why? Simply because the armed struggle clearly is interrelated with the uprising which took place in December. Such uprisings are bound to reoccur. If Russia is considered as a whole, then this relationship [between armed struggle and armed uprising] is not so clearly noticeable, but it does exist. After all, there is no question but that "partisan" struggle reached its greatest popularity after the December rising. Those actions are related not only to the economic crisis but also to the political crisis. Traditional Russian terrorism was the work of plotting intellectuals. Now, workers or unemployed persons who are members of combat groups usually are leading this struggle.[14] People who like to generalize according to abstract patterns easily may think of anarchism or Blanquism. In the face of an insurrectionist situation as it clearly existed in the Lettish area, such phrases learned by rote obviously are meaningless.

The Lettish example demonstrates that the usual method of analyzing partisan action without regard to the status of the uprising is completely wrong, unscientific and unhistorical. The [concrete] situation must be taken into consideration. The characteristics of the transition periods between large uprisings must be taken into account. The types of struggle which, in a given period, are becoming inevitable should not be criticized with a few clichés such as anarchism, plunder, and *Lumpenproletariat*, as is customary among Cadets[15] and the *Novoye Vremya* crowd.

It is said that partisan actions disorganize our work. Let us see to what extent this evaluation is justified, especially with respect to the period after December 1905 and to the areas under martial law and [suffering from] Black Hundreds pogroms. What is it that disorganizes the movement in such an area more: the lack of resistance or the lack of [a well] organized partisan struggle? Compare the situation in Central Russia with that of the Western border regions, such as Poland and Livonia. There is no doubt that in the Western provinces partisan struggles occur far more frequently and have reached a higher stage of development. Contrariwise, there is no doubt that in Central Russia the revolutionary movement in general, and the social democratic movement in particular, is far *more disorganized* [than in the West]. Certainly we would not think of concluding that because of the partisan struggle the Polish and Lettish social democratic movement has suffered from disorganization less [than the movement in Central Russia]. No. The point is merely that the partisan struggle is not responsible for the disorganization of the Russian social democratic workers movement [which occurred] during 1906.

In this connection, frequent reference has been made to the peculiarities of national conditions. Such arguments disclose the weakness of the customary objections to partisan struggle. If it is a matter of national conditions, then obviously it is not a matter of anarchism, Blanquism, or terrorism, but something else is involved: general Russian or even specifically Russian sins. Analyze this "something else" more *concretely*, gentlemen! You will find that national oppression or national antagonisms explain nothing. These conditions always were present in the Western border regions, yet partisan actions have occurred only in a special historical period. There are many regions where national oppression and antagonisms have been rampant, and yet no partisan struggles are taking place. The fact is that sometimes partisan struggles develop in the absence of any national oppression.[16] A concrete analysis of this question would show that it is not national oppression but the development of the uprising which is decisive. Partisan struggle is an unavoidable form of action at a time when the mass movement has matured to the point of insurrection and when the intervals between the "big battles" of the civil war are becoming shorter.

The movement has not been disorganized by partisan struggles but by the weakness of the party, which does not know how to *take those actions into its own hands.* Consequently, the indictments against partisan warfare, so customary among us Russians, go together with secret, accidental, and unorganized partisan actions which, indeed, do disorganize the party. If we do not understand the historical conditions of partisan warfare, then we shall be unable to eliminate its darker sides. In spite of everything, partisan operations occur [because they] are created by powerful economic and political causes. Since we are unable to get rid of those causes, we are unable to prevent this type of struggle. Our complaints about partisan warfare are nothing but complaints about the weakness of our party [which is incapable of] organizing the uprising.

What we said about disorganization also applies to demoralization. Partisan struggle as such does not produce demoralization, which results rather from *disorganization,* undisciplined armed actions, and from lack of party leadership. Demoralization, which *unquestionably* has set in, cannot be overcome by disapproving and rejecting the [concept of] partisan struggle. Such censures are by no means sufficient to prevent events which result from profound economic and political causes. It could be objected that, while we may not have the capability of suppressing abnormal and demoralizing happenings, no purpose would be served if the party were to use anomalous and demoralizing tactics. Such a non-Marxist objection would be of a purely liberal-bourgeois character. No Marxist should consider partisan warfare, which is just one of the forms of civil war, as abnormal and demoralizing. Marxists favor class struggle and not social peace. In periods of grave economic and political crisis, the class struggle develops into civil war—that is, into an armed struggle between two parts of the people. In such periods, every Marxist is *obliged* to endorse the cause of civil war. From the Marxist point of view, moral condemnations of civil war are entirely unacceptable.

In situations of civil war, a *combat party* is the ideal type of a proletarian party. This is indisputable. We admit that one may try to prove, and perhaps may be able to prove, the inadvisability of this or that type of struggle at this or that juncture of the civil war. From the point of view of *military expediency*, criticism of the various forms of civil war certainly is justified. We agree that the decisive voice in such questions belongs to those experienced socialist leaders who are familiar with the practical conditions in each locality. But, in the name of Marxist principles, we must insist that civil war be analyzed seriously and that shopworn phrases such as anarchism, Blanquism, and terrorism not be thrown into the debate. Senseless partisan actions, such as were indulged in by this or that organization of the PPS[17] in this or that situation, should not be abused for a scare argument against socialist participation in partisan warfare.

One must accept assertions that partisan warfare disorganizes the [socialist] movement with skepticism. *Every* new form of struggle which involves new dangers and new sacrifices inevitably will "disorganize" organizations unprepared for the new tactics. Our old study groups became disorganized when agitational methods were adopted. Later on, our party committees were disorganized when the party took to demonstrations. In every war, new tactics carry a degree of disorganization into the battle ranks. Yet this is no argument against fighting a war. It merely follows that one must *learn* how to wage war. That is all there is to it.

When I meet social democrats who proudly and self-righteously declare, "we are no anarchists, no thieves, no robbers, we are above [such violent forms of struggle], we reject partisan warfare," then I ask myself: "Do these people understand what they are talking about?" Violent incidents and armed clashes between the Black Hundreds government and the people are happening all over the country. This is inevitable at the present stage of revolution. The population reacts to the attacks by Black Hundreds troopers with armed *coups de main* and ambushes. Because they are spontaneous and unorganized, these counterattacks may assume inexpedient and *evil* forms. I understand quite well that, due to weakness and lack of preparation by our organization, the party may refrain from assuming, at given places and times, the leadership of such spontaneous actions. I understand that this question must be decided by local practitioners and that the strengthening of weak and unprepared party organizations is not an easy task. But if a social democratic theoretician or writer fails to be saddened by such lack of preparedness and, on the contrary, displays proud self-satisfaction, and conceitedly and enthusiastically repeats slogans on anarchism, Blanquism, and terrorism which he memorized in his early youth, then I consider this to be a degradation of the world's most revolutionary doctrine.

It is asserted that partisan actions lower the class-conscious proletariat to the level of drunkards and bums. This is correct. But from this follows only that the party of the proletariat never should consider partisan warfare to be its only or even its chief means of struggle. This particular technique must be integrated with other tactics and be in harmony with the most important methods of combat. Partisan warfare should be ennobled by the enlightening and organizing influence of socialism. Without this *last* condition, *all*—clearly all—means of struggle will move the proletariat [which lives] within a bourgeois society close to various nonproletarian strata, whether they stand higher or lower [in social rank].[18] If they are allowed to develop spontaneously, such techniques will lose their effectiveness and their original form and will become prostituted.[19] Strikes which are left to take a spontaneous course degenerate into "alliances," i.e., agreements between business and labor *against* the consumer. Parliament becomes a brothel where gangs of bourgeois politicians are bargaining, wholesale and retail, about "people's freedom," "liberalism," "democracy," republicanism, anti-clericalism, socialism, and other brands of popular commodities. Newspapers turn into cheap procurers and into tools corrupting the masses and flattering the lowest mob instincts, etc. The socialists know of no universally applicable combat method which would separate the proletariat, as though by a Chinese wall, from those classes of the people which [socially] are situated slightly higher or slightly lower. Socialists use different means at different periods. Those means are chosen in *strict* accordance with ideological and organizational conditions the nature of which must be determined *accurately* [by the Marxist dialectic method].

The bolsheviks[20] have been accused frequently of an unthinking party-oriented [and positive] attitude toward partisan actions. It seems necessary, therefore, to reiterate that the *particular* bolshevik faction[21] which approved partisan warfare defined in its draft [of a social democratic party resolution] the conditions under which armed struggle would be permissible: "Expropriations" of private property are entirely forbidden. "Expropriations" of government property are not recommended, but are *permitted* provided they are accomplished *under party control* and provided the captured money is used for the *purposes of the uprising*. Terrorist partisan acts against representatives of the violent regime and of *active* Black Hundreds groups *are recommended*[22] but are subject to the following restrictions: (1) the popular mood must be taken into account; (2) local conditions under which the workers movement is operating must be considered; (3) care must be taken that no proletarian forces are wasted unnecessarily. The *only* practical difference between the resolution accepted by the unification congress of the [Social Democratic] Party[23] and our draft resolution is that [in the former] "expropriations" of government property were entirely forbidden.

IV

The Russian revolution differs from bourgeois revolutions in Europe in that it displays an immense variety in the methods of struggle. Kautsky predicted this in 1902, at least to a point, when he said that the coming revolution (and he added: *perhaps* with the exception of Russia) will not be so much a struggle of the people against the government as a struggle of one part of the people against the other. In Russia we witnessed a broader development of the *second* kind of struggle than during the bourgeois revolutions in the West. The enemies of our revolution have but few followers among the people, but as the fight develops the opponents are getting better and better organized and are gaining support from reactionary groups of the bourgeoisie. Thus, it is natural and unavoidable that in *such* periods, in a period of political general strikes, *the uprising* cannot assume the traditional form of a single blow, limited to a very short time and a very small area.[24] [Under such circumstances], it is natural and unavoidable that the uprising assumes the higher and more complicated form of a protracted civil war enmeshing the entire country—that is, the form of armed struggle by one part of the people against the other. Such a war must be conceived as a series of a few big battles, separated by comparatively long intervals, and a large number of small engagements which take place during these interim periods. If this is so—and it undoubtedly is so—then the task of social democracy is to create organizations most suitable to leading the masses both in the big battles and, so far as practical, in the smaller actions. At a time when the class struggle is developing into civil war, social democrats must consider it their task not only to *participate* in this civil war, but must play the leading role in this conflict. The Social Democratic Party must educate and prepare its organizations in such a way that they will become true belligerents who will not fail to exploit opportunities through which the strengths of the opponent can be sapped.

Unquestionably, this is a difficult task. It cannot be accomplished at once. Similarly, as an entire people is transforming itself in the course of civil war and is learning from the struggle, so our organizations, if they are to fulfill their mission, must be educated and reorganized on the basis of experience.

We do not presume at all to impose on comrades who are carrying on with their practical work any theoretical ideas about tactics, let alone to decide from the vantage point of a desk what role this or that form of partisan struggle should assume during the civil war in Russia. We shall not confuse particular *political orientations* within the social democratic movement with specific partisan actions.[25] But we consider it our task to provide a correct *theoretical* evaluation of the new forms of struggle which life has created.[26] Our business is to fight pitilessly against the clichés and prejudices which are hindering the class-conscious workers from posing a new and difficult question in the right manner and hence from solving it correctly.

A VIET CONG DIRECTIVE ON "REPRESSION" 2

After eight years of conflict, the First Indochina War came to an end when agreements were reached at an international conference held in Geneva in 1954. As a result of the accords, independence was granted to Laos and Cambodia as well as to both the northern and southern sections of Viet Nam, which was partitioned along the 17th parallel, North Viet Nam was Communist; South Viet Nam was not.

The Geneva agreements called for the holding of elections both in the North and the South in 1956, and the Communists hoped that the voting would serve to unify the country under their banner. South Viet Nam had not signed the agreements, however, and it refused to hold elections. The Communists turned to hostile methods in their effort to take over that country.

A clandestine Communist apparatus had been maintained in the South. A substantial number of other Communist party members traveled to the North to receive training in terror and guerrilla tactics. These members were then infiltrated back into the South. Weapons left over from the war against the French had been stored for future use.

The launching of terrorist activities in South Viet Nam in 1957 signaled the start of the Communist attempt to subjugate that country. The terror was directed at destroying the governmental fabric of control in the rural areas. Village chiefs, policemen, teachers, priests, and other locally important figures were the targets of Communist assassins. In 1957, it has been estimated, one civilian was killed every other day.[1] By 1960 that figure was up to five per day.[2] The number continued rising, and deaths by terror occur to this day. How many people have been killed by Viet Cong terrorists? No one has a precise number, but it clearly runs into the tens of thousands.

The Viet Cong utilize terror as part of their campaign of conquest, and they also use it in order to maintain control of areas they have taken over. The following Viet Cong directive, captured by troops of the U.S. First Air Cavalry Division, sets forth Communist views and instructions on "repressing counter-revolutionary elements" in "areas under our own control" and in "areas temporarily under enemy control."

The directive specifically cites as "targets" for repression" the following persons: "Spies and secret agents . . ." "Cruel elements in the enemy armed forces . . ." "Elements in oppressive organizations . . ." "Elements who actively fight against the Revolution in reactionary parties . . ." "Reactionary and recalcitrant elements who take advantage of various religions . . ." "All other recalcitrant and reactionary elements who are actively opposing the Revolution." The phraseology is familiar. The Communists label as enemies of "the Revolution" those people who are considered to be the greatest threat to Communist plans. Such persons, and especially policemen and political and religious figures, must be eliminated.

In areas under Viet Cong control, death sentences are to be meted out to "cruel instigators, extremely reactionary elements, ringleaders with an acute hatred of the Revolution, and those dangerous henchmen who have committed serious crimes who are hated by the people and are beyond reform."

In areas under government control, the Viet Cong are "to exterminate dangerous and cruel elements such as security agents, policemen, and other cruel elements in espionage organizations, professional secret agents in organizations to counter the Revolution, henchmen with many blood debts in village administrative machines, in the puppet system, in enemy military and paramilitary organizations, and key and dangerous members" of opposition parties.

The directive does admit, however, that excessive terrorism has redounded against the Viet Cong. It states, "We arrest people arbitrarily," and, "Judgments are not made seriously and prudently." Furthermore, "There are many cases in which innocent people are killed and, at certain places, some people have been executed savagely." The result, says the directive, is that "these mistakes not only have a bad influence on relations between the Party and [National Liberation] Front and the people but also affect unity in rural areas."

The directive does not question the merits of terror; it only urges more care in the selection of victims. Viet Cong thinking echoes a statement once made by Lenin. "Do you really think that we shall be victorious without using the most cruel terror?"[3]

DIRECTIVE

Concerning a number of problems that require thorough understanding in Z's[4] task of repressing counterrevolutionary elements.

I. *A Summary of Past Repression Activities*

Based on the spirit and subject of instructions from higher echelons, F.102 [Military Region 5 HQ] on 9 December 1962 issued Directive No. 49 containing guidelines on realizing our policy for repressing counterrevolutionary elements. In early May 1965 another directive was issued to complement the former one.

Accordingly, party committees have made great efforts and achieved positive results in the task of realizing the policy, reinforcing the repression of counterrevolutionary elements, and rectifying mistakes and shortcomings.

In regard to the task of motivating the people, we have indoctrinated and reformed thousands of people who rashly committed crimes against the Revolution, punished a number of the enemy's recalcitrant henchmen who opposed and attacked the Revolution, disintegrated many reactionary political organizations and secret networks of the enemy in rural areas, and thus have made timely contributions to the task of destroying strategic hamlets, winning over the people and consolidating our position as masters. We have also achieved progress in the educational field and have succeeded in drawing the attention of more people to our policy. The executive organization that has carried out the policy has also progressed.

The above-mentioned achievements have had the effect of preventing and limiting enemy sabotage activities and have decimated the ranks of enemy henchmen, thus contributing to the task of consolidating the movement, holding firm and developing the liberated areas, and creating more favorable conditions to step up revolutionary activity and realize the Party's policies.

However, we still commit many mistakes in our task of repressing counterrevolutionary elements and still suffer from many shortcomings, especially since large areas in rural lowlands have been liberated. The struggle between us and our enemies is being conducted in a fierce manner. As we face new plots and stratagems of the enemy, our mistakes assume a more serious, widespread, and extensive nature and include facts such as the following:

—We arrest people arbitrarily. In certain cases, the offenses of those arrested have not been confirmed and some persons arrested have not deserved to be arrested (doubtful cases, [those guilty only of] minor offenses in daily routines). There are also cases where the reasons leading to arrest are not correct (personal vengeance, etc.).

—The organization of detention is still poor and, at certain places, detainees suffer from malnutrition, illness, and lack of clothing. Many places pay excessive attention to required labor and production and neglect the task of educating, reforming, and eradicating the reactionary thought [of prisoners]. Torture and third-degree interrogation are still used. At certain places, jails even exist at the village level.

—Judgments are not made seriously and prudently. Too many people are arrested and punished. There is no discrimination between detaining people pending judgment and forcing them to undergo thought reform or on-the-spot education. Efforts have not yet been made to conduct public trials to announce sentence and the time necessary for reform. At the present time, the ratio of people assassinated in the liberated areas is too high. There are many cases in which innocent people are killed and, at certain places, some people have been executed savagely.

—Principles pertaining to judgment and approval are not absolutely respected, especially at the district and village levels.

Aside from this, there are also signs of rightism, such as lack of vigilance, lack of determination, and lack of timely measures. We also fail to uncover and actively track down covert enemies and strike properly at the ringleaders; thus we still allow dangerous enemy henchmen to escape and continue to oppose and attack us. We also have permitted enemy spies and reactionary elements to infiltrate into and operate within our areas of control.

In brief, we can say that our task of repressing counterrevolutionary elements has not yet been carried out in an absolute, determined, and cautious manner.

These are mistakes and shortcomings pertaining to the policy and line on repressing counterrevolutionary elements, and contrary to both absolute and democratic principles. These mistakes not only have a bad influence on relations between the Party and Front and the people but also affect unity in the rural areas. They cause the people to feel anxious and are detrimental to the task of concentrating all forces to fight against the Americans for our national salvation. They may have major and lasting consequences and create opportunities by which the enemy can profit.

The Reasons [for Our Mistakes] Are:

—We have not been determined in our class standpoint and still fail to distinguish the boundary that separates our enemy from ourselves, and we have not yet thoroughly understood democratic absolutism. Therefore, in regard to the enemy, we have failed to launch our attacks at the right moment, against the right persons and the right crimes. With regard to the people, we have transgressed their free and democratic rights and have taken the lives of many persons who did not deserve a death sentence. In addition, we have shown signs of thought confusion, failing to be vigilant enough in ordinary times, then when difficulties arise becoming confused and arresting the wrong persons and pronouncing the wrong sentences. Certain comrades among us think that arresting people will solve all problems and constitute a basic solution, but, on the contrary, this actually creates more complications and difficulties.

—We have not yet thoroughly understood the policy for repressing counterrevolutionary elements and in our past activities we have had to coordinate it with related policies. We have failed to apply the spirit of being firm in principles and flexible in practice. We have not paid attention to the special nature of the situation at given times and have not understood that the political requirements and the requirements of repressing counterrevolutionary elements call for striking at one person to shake, put down, and prevent [the activities of] many others.

—We do not lean completely on the people and put confidence in the people. On the other hand, we are inclined to court the people and to lack sufficient determination to persuade the people, explain the Party's policy, and enable them to understand it clearly.

—Party Committees have not thoroughly and specifically led in the task of repressing counterrevolutionaries and have failed to control, rectify, and make necessary corrections in a timely manner. Concepts of organization and discipline and sense of responsibility have not been promoted, especially at district and village levels.

II. *A Number of Problems That Require Thorough Understanding in the Task of Repressing Counterrevolutionary Elements*

The task of suppressing reactionary elements is being carried out while we are fighting against the Americans for our national salvation

and also in a very complicated political situation which has these noticeable characteristics:

—By the nature of this special war, the U.S. imperialists are leaning on the puppet troops and government to take active advantage of
various religions, maintain reactionary political parties, and use cunning and stealthy plots to induce a great number of people to work for
them.

But among the people who are working for or have relations with the
enemy, there are only a few who have dangerously reactionary minds
and interests that oppose the Revolution and bind them to the imperialists and recalcitrant elements which are strongly against the Revolution.
The majority are people who are forced to work for the enemy or
bought over or people who have temporarily gone astray and committed
crimes against the Revolution.

—Our people have been under the enemy's grip for years; thus they
feel acute hatred for the aggressors and the clique of henchmen. Now
that they are strongly rising up to secure the role of masters, they are
eager to take part in repressing counterrevolutionaries, but they will
surely commit mistakes if they do not have the Party's guidance. We
must also consider the fact that our people have been indoctrinated by
the enemy for a long time, and we must take it as our duty to distinguish
between backward and reactionary thought.

—We do not yet have a thoroughly organized government and clear-
cut laws while we must build a democratic regime in a war situation in
which the conflict is growing fiercer and fiercer and our enemies are employing many spies and crafty propaganda means. Moreover, the situation of the various parties and religions is also very complicated. There is
no [formal] demarcation line between our zone and that of our enemies
[but] the requirements for repressing counterrevolutionaries differ in
areas newly acquired and mastered, in disputed areas, and temporarily
occupied areas; even in the liberated areas the situations in the lowland
and the highlands are different. Thus the question of properly carrying
out the policy of repressing counterrevolutionary elements in each place
and at each time is not a simple one.

The Revolution is rising while the enemy is weakening, and the liberated areas are growing larger and larger. We have the opportunity to
motivate the people and lean on them to educate and reform the guilty
elements, discover and punish cruel henchmen, etc.

On the basis of these points and from past experience fighting counterrevolutionaries, F.102 specifically prescribes the following:

A. Targets for Repression

The targets for repression are counterrevolutionary elements who seek to impede the Revolution and work actively for the enemy and for destruction of the Revolution.

The targets for repression now consist of the following main categories of persons:

(1) Spies and secret agents of the Americans, the puppet government, and capitalist and imperialist countries such as: France, Japan, etc., including spies operating in disguised espionage organizations, such as malaria control, rural pacification, and mobile administration teams.

(2) Cruel elements in the enemy armed forces and paramilitary forces.

(3) Elements in oppressive organizations and in the puppet ranks who actively oppose and seek to destroy the Revolution.

(4) Elements who actively fight against the Revolution in reactionary parties such as the Vietnamese Nationalist Party (Quoc Dan Dang), Party for a Greater Viet Nam (Dai-Viet), and Personality and Labor Party (Can-Lao Nhan-Vi), and key reactionaries in organizations and associations founded by the reactionary parties or the U.S. imperialists and the puppet government.

(5) Reactionary and recalcitrant elements who take advantage of various religions, such as Catholicism, Buddhism, Caodaism and Protestantism, actively to oppose and destroy the Revolution, and key elements in organizations and associations founded by these persons.

(6) All other recalcitrant and reactionary elements who are actively opposing the Revolution.

These are the counterrevolutionary targets which we must repress and punish. But how are we to repress and punish them? By detaining them, forcing them to attend reform sessions, imprisoning them, or sentencing them to death. Whatever form of punishment we use must take into consideration political factors, the requirements for repression, the seriousness of the crimes committed, and the attitude toward repentance of each of the defendants. Concurrently, we must also take into consideration related policies, such as the Front policy, land policy, military proselyting policy, religious policy, minority people policy, etc., so as to make judgments in a prudent and serious manner.

B. Specific Policy

The policy on repressing counterrevolutionaries consists of: *"Combining repression with clemency, combining punishment with education and reform; sternly punishing cruel ringleaders and recalcitrant elements who oppose and strive to destroy the Revolution; being lenient toward people who show sincere repentance, people who have gone astray, or people who were forced to act as they did; allowing for extenuating circumstances and forgiving those who redeem themselves by making contributions to the revolution, and rewarding those who make outstanding contributions."*

To carry out this policy correctly, we must observe absolutely the principle of *"leaning on the people and coordinating the activeness of the people with the professional guidance of specialized organizations under the leadership of the Party."* We must thoroughly understand the motto, *"Promote vigilance, allow no wrongdoer to escape, avoid committing mistakes, and misjudge no one."* We must also cultivate the spirit of being *"determined, cautious, serious, firm in principles but flexible in practice."*

In the present situation, we must direct the thrust of our punishment toward active henchmen of the U.S. imperialists who have committed many crimes and are inflicting many losses upon our people and the Revolution; then we must strive to educate a great number of other people who have been forced to serve the enemy, who have gone astray, or have been bought over. Our objective is to parry the thrust, isolate, disintegrate, weaken, and disperse the enemy ranks and actively maintain and develop our forces correctly to serve the immediate and the long-range political missions, which include specifically:

   1. In areas under our own control:
      Imprisonment and death sentences:

(1) Sentence to a term of imprisonment varying from ten to twenty years or to death all elements who are serving as enemy henchmen and who are actively and fiercely opposing and striving to destroy the revolution and are perpetrating many crimes and creating much damage to the local revolutionary movement.

Death sentences must be strictly limited: Death sentences are to be applied only to cruel instigators, extremely reactionary elements, ringleaders with an acute hatred of the Revolution, and those dangerous henchmen who have committed serious crimes who are hated by the people and are beyond reform.

Sentence to less than ten years of imprisonment all reactionary elements and enemy henchmen who are opposing the Revolution and are doing harm to the people and the Revolution but whose crimes are light or who, even though their crimes are serious, show certain signs of repentance.

(2) Forced participation in group thought reform sessions: Force to attend group thought reform sessions for three months all elements which have collaborated with the enemy and committed certain crimes, including fairly serious crimes, but have confessed. This measure applies also to persons who formerly served or still are serving the enemy and have just been discovered by us but whose crimes still are insignificant.

The duration of thought reform can be increased, but only once and not more than three months.

At the end of the period of thought reform, if a subject remains recalcitrant and continues to oppose the Revolution, then he must be judged by a court.

(3) House arrest: Keep under house arrest in local areas for a period of two years all elements who refuse to be reformed, those who have been released from prison but are not truly repentant, those who are suspected of having relations with the enemy or serving him secretly and whose crimes do not yet warrant their arrest.

Depending upon the attitude and behavior of each person under house arrest, the duration of house arrest may be either increased or decreased, but it can be increased only once and for not more than six months.

At the end of a period of house arrest, if the detainee shows no signs of progress or keeps on working for the enemy, then he must be judged by a court.

Sentences prescribing the confiscation of land and surrendering of properties must be carried out in accordance with F.102's directive on the realization of the land policy.

2. In areas temporarily under enemy control:

(1) We are to exterminate dangerous and cruel elements such as security agents, policemen, and other cruel elements in espionage organizations, professional secret agents in organizations to counter the Revolution, henchmen with many blood debts [to us] in village administrative machines, in the puppet system, in enemy military and paramilitary organizations, and key and dangerous members of such parties as the Vietnamese Nationalist Party, the Party for a Greater Viet Nam, and the Personality and Labor Party.

(2) We are to establish files immediately and prepare the ground for later suppression of dangerous henchmen whom we need not eliminate yet or whose elimination is not yet politically advantageous.

Files must also be established on counterrevolutionary elements sent abroad by the enemy and those who have committed many crimes and gone into exile in foreign countries.

While applying the above-mentioned regulations, we must observe the following:

—Distinguish areas temporarily occupied by the enemy from areas in which we are the masters; distinguish the elimination of tyrants and local administrative personnel while fighting from the continuous task of repressing counterrevolutionaries in the liberated areas.

—Distinguish the ringleaders, the commissioned officers, from the henchmen.

—Distinguish the exploiting elements from the basic elements and distinguish persons determined to oppose the Revolution from those who are forced to do so or who are bought over and have no political understanding.

—Distinguish between persons with much political and religious influence and those who have no influence or very little influence.

—Distinguish between historical problems and present day problems.

—Distinguish major crimes with many bad effects from minor crimes or innocence.

—Distinguish determined and stubborn antirevolutionary attitudes from attitudes of submission to the Revolution and true repentance, and willingness to redeem by contribution to the Revolution.

—Distinguish counterrevolutionary elements from backward and dissatisfied persons among the masses.

3. Principles pertaining to detention and judgment
   a. *Arrest*

(1) A file clearly stating the crimes committed is required for each arrest.

(2) Arrests in the areas in which we are masters and in disputed areas must be approved by the Current Affairs Committee of the Provincial Party Committee and ordered by the province security agency.

Arrests may be made during combat without approval from higher echelons, but a file must be established later and the arrest must be reported to the province level.

Whenever someone is caught in the act [of committing a crime], any person has the right to arrest him and take him to the authorities.

(3) Arrest of special targets such as well known men, intellectuals, religious leaders, and public leaders of ethnic minority groups must be

approved by the Current Affairs Committee of the Regional Party Committee and ordered by the regional security agency.

b. *Detention*

(1) Districts and provinces are allowed to organize detention camps, [but] villages may not maintain such camps and are not allowed to detain [prisoners], make use of third degree interrogations, or force people to attend reform sessions.

(2) District detention camps are for detainees only [suspects held for interrogation]. Provincial detention camps are for both detainees and convicted prisoners. Detainees must be kept separate [from the convicts]. Men are to be separated from the women, and detainees from convicts. Major criminals, minor criminals, and persons who are forced to attend reform sessions must also be separated.

Special treatment must be provided for persons who are forced to join thought reform concentration centers.

Special targets can be detained only in provincial jails.

(3) During detention, interrogations must be conducted quickly and detainees must not be forced to make depositions; torture is strictly forbidden, including mental torture. Detention time must not exceed three months.

(4) Evidence in the case, properties, personal belongings of the culprits must be properly preserved and protected from illegal violation.

(5) Coordinate political education and thought struggle with forced labor and production for self sufficiency to reduce the expenses of the Revolution and transform detention camps into genuine reform and control centers.

c. *Judgment*

(1) All arrested persons shall be judged publicly and a verdict shall be pronounced for each of them.

District level has the right to pronounce sentences of from one to three years, but it must obtain prior approval from the Current Affairs Committee of the Provincial Party Committee.

Province has the right to pronounce sentences from three years up.

Judgment of special targets, such as puppet field grade officers and puppet province chiefs, and the delivery of a death sentence must be approved in advance by the Current Affairs Committee of the Regional Party Committee.

A sentence to imprisonment will not be subject to appeal. After each trial, a copy of the sentence must be sent to the guilty party's local area for information [of the authorities there].

(2) Culprits may benefit from extenuating circumstances or amnesties on proposal by the echelon handling the judgment subject to approval by the next higher echelon (provincial authorities can decide on extenuation or amnesty on judgments handed down by district authorities).

(3) Severely restrict secret executions and carry out all death sentences in a serious manner. Savage executions are strictly forbidden.

(4) Set up revolutionary people's courts publicly to judge culprits, although, depending on the situation, the participation of a large number of people is not necessarily required for all trial sessions.

While a system of law courts is still unavailable, security agencies have the mission of guiding and organizing trial sessions. District and Provincial Party Committees are to assume direct leadership and assign cadres to serve as presiding judges and judges, and security cadres to serve as public prosecutors and court registrars.

A revolutionary people's court will be summoned when the situation requires. After the completion of its mission, it will be dismissed.

III. *Organization and Realization*

Organize sessions for thorough study of this directive throughout our Party. This directive must be studied by cadres from regional to district commissar levels, and key cadres from all branches of a district, with a view toward heightening their revolutionary understanding, maintaining and correctly carrying out the Party's policy and control, and planning to rectify all mistakes committed in their areas. Only the specific and main points and principles of this directive and not the entire directive are to be disseminated to lower level cadres and Party members. As for the people, particular public documents]relative to this directive[shall be made available.

Party schools and political training courses shall use this directive as a document to educate people in the policy of repressing counterrevolutionary elements.

On the basis of this directive, cadres of all levels shall thoroughly check on past activities in repressing counterrevolutionaries, organize and control the activities of lower levels in carrying out this task, require responsible branches to uncover all mistakes and shortcomings and, on that basis, rectify such deficiencies with a firm and fearless determination. We must prevent one mistake from leading to another.

After completion of the study and bringing our efforts under control, those who still commit serious mistakes and fail to carry out exactly the prescribed policy shall be subjected to serious criticism and appropriate discipline and their failures must be reported to F.102. Security and training agencies have the mission of helping Party Committees to carry out this directive. Previous directives contrary to this one are rescinded.

24 December 1965
F.102

THE PALESTINIAN TERRORISTS: STATEMENTS BY YASSER ARAFAT AND WILLIAM KHOURY

3

Three times in recent years, in 1948-49, in 1956 (in alliance with France and Great Britain), and in 1967, Israel has defeated neighboring Arab countries. Each of these conflicts has been a conventional war, with the Israelis relying heavily on tank thrusts and air strikes to achieve their victories.

Over a million refugees fled Israel during this period of turbulence. In the refugee camps where these Palestinians lived, militant groups were organized and their members were trained and armed. Under way for years in a desultory manner, this military preparation was stepped up determinedly following the 1967 conflict.

Recognizing that unconventional warfare was their best strategy, the Palestinians began utilizing guerrilla and terror tactics against the Israelis. The irregulars, sanctioned and assisted in varying degrees by several of the Arab countries, staged raids across the borders, set off bombs, and shot at Israeli soldiers. The fact that Israel had occupied substantial portions of Arab territory in the 1967 war enabled the militants to establish clandestine movements among the populations of those areas. (The Israelis were not unfamiliar with terrorism. They had utilized it in their own struggle for independence from the British.)

The Palestinians staged border raids. The Israelis retaliated with counterblows of their own. The Palestinians carried out terror acts. The

Israelis replied by burning down the homes of persons believed to be helping the terrorists. The crescendo of conflict increased to the point that Israel and its neighbors were virtually at war once again. Adding an especially ominous note was the fact that the United States was committed to assisting Israel and the Soviet Union was committed to Egypt, militarily the main Arab nation. Faced with the stark reality that events might well lead to a direct confrontation between the two superpowers, the various involved nations arranged a ceasefire, and this went into effect on 7 August 1970.

The Palestinian organizations, however, refused to accept the ceasefire. Their activities were nevertheless largely restrained by the Arab governments—in Jordan it took an all-out drive by the army to subdue the guerrillas.

In interviews and statements Palestinian leaders have explained what they hope to accomplish through the use of terrorism. One of the leaders is George Habash, a medical doctor who heads a militant group called the Popular Front for the Liberation of Palestine. In an interview Habash explained the rationale behind terrorist activities by his organization. His words expressed the thinking of clandestine groups everywhere that rely primarily on terror tactics in order to combat a more powerful foe. Asked, "What is heroic about striking a hospital or blowing up an airplane?," he replied:

> It's guerrilla warfare, a special kind of guerrilla warfare. The main point is to select targets where success is 100% assured. To harass, to upset, to work on the nerves. . . . You should see how my people react to a successful operation! Spirit shoots sky-high.[1]

Terrorism, in effect, is a form of psychological warfare. As Habash stated, it is a type of guerrilla combat: a wearing away of the strong by the weak. Habash echoed the thinking of Mao Tse-tung, Vo Nguyen Giap, and Ernesto Guevara when he declared: "The only way to destroy [the enemy] is to give a little blow here, a little blow there; to advance step by step, inch by inch, for years, for decades, with determination, doggedness, patience."[2]

There follow excerpts from statements by Yasser Arafat, leader of the Al Fatah militant organization, and by William Khoury, Syrian delegate to the Organization of Solidarity of the Peoples of Africa, Asia, and Latin America, a Cuban-sponsored propaganda and subversive organism. Heavily larded with propaganda, these statements nevertheless convey the strategy behind the Palestinian terrorist campaign. Again the influence of Mao, Giap, and Guevara is evident. Arafat refers to a "long-term war" which will lead to "enemy exhaustion through continuous operations." The Palestinians are to use "special tactics" (a fine euphemism for terrorism) and targets are to be civilian as well as military. The underground movement develops into a military fighting force, just as rural guerrillas, if they are successful, develop into regular military forces.

Khoury, in his statement, emphasizes the use of "armed struggle" and states that this is "the only possible solution" to the Palestinian question. The Palestinians, says Khoury, are to follow "the road taken by the heroic Vietnamese people in their struggle against U.S. imperialism." Just as Guevara hoped to create several "Viet Nams" in Latin America, the Palestinians believe the Mid East, too, can be converted by terrorism into a new Viet Nam.

YASSER ARAFAT
Commander of Al Fatah

Our people have been waging a fierce battle for more than fifty years. Our struggle was against Zionist settlement, first adopted and supported by British colonialism and then by international imperialism headed by the United States. In 1948, the majority of our people were uprooted and forced into refugee camps. The Palestine Liberation Movement began among these refugees in the late fifties. At last we carried out our first military operation precisely in the first hour of 1965. Since then we have continued our struggle in action and will continue it until our entire homeland has been liberated.

After having been expelled from their land and tortured, the Palestinian people expected justice from the whole world, represented in the United Nations, but nothing happened. So they have no other alternative but to fight to regain their homeland.

The UN charter gives all peoples the right to self-determination. Not only are we deprived of this right, but of our country itself. So every Palestinian, wherever he is, is a victim of the same injustice practiced against him. This feeling was the common motive for all Palestinians to regain their identity, their nationality, and their homeland through armed struggle. Since we are facing an enemy supported by imperialist funds and technical achievements, we have chosen long-term war as the strategy for our struggle. Through this long war all our people can participate, since they have nothing to lose but their tents and their misery.

As for the enemy, the importance of this strategy is to eliminate the gap in his army between relaxation and readiness. In this we have had considerable success. This leads to enemy exhaustion through continuous operations, whether by attacking military and industrial targets or by destroying shipping lines wherever they are. Finally comes the stage of liberation of areas on the way to total liberation.

To achieve this we must use special tactics. These tactics are not static, we have to change them continuously to meet the requirements of the stage of our liberation war.

When the revolution started, the Palestinians did not ask anybody's permission. The revolution depends entirely on the Palestinians, whether for the recruitment of fighters or for financial support. We represent the aspirations of the Palestinians; for this reason, they have joined us willingly.

Al Fatah started as an underground movement because we were not allowed to operate freely from any Arab territory.

.   .   .

The turning point in our struggle was the battle of El Karamah. Since then we have been challenging the enemy in similar confrontations because we are aware of the great value of the human element compared to the enemy's war machinery.

Through these stages we have developed our combat capacity, increased our numbers, organized political cells, and achieved more efficient training.

The final goal of what is called the political solution is nothing less than to return to the situation as it was before that war. This simply means that we have to carry on our struggle until our country is totally liberated. Revolutionaries, as you know, do not bargain.

.   .   .

WILLIAM KHOURY
Delegate to the O.S.P.A.A.L.

I n the face of . . . barbarous [Israeli] acts, it was natural for the Palestinians to put up a legal resistance to defend their very existence.

The Al Fatah organization, which heads the Palestinian armed struggle against the Israeli occupation, is continually consolidating its positions, accelerating this just struggle, at the same that the support of the masses and of the Arab governments as well as the admiration and support of progressive world public opinion for this organization is increasing.

It is well known today, both by the Arab people and all the Palestinian people that there is no other solution to the Israel question than the armed struggle, since Israel persists in its policy of invasion and merciless racist occupation.

The Al Fatah, Al Saika and the PFPL (Popular Front for Palestinian Liberation) organization have dealt mortal blows to the Zionist occupants; they have waged hundreds of battles in the interior of occupied Palestine. Moshe Dayan, the Israeli Minister of Defense, was forced to admit that Israeli losses since the 5 June 1967 war have mounted to more than 1,600 soldiers.

The intensity of the Palestinian armed struggle has reached such a degree that the United States has had to send experts in guerrilla warfare to try, in vain, to crush the struggle of the Palestinian commandos. U.S. observers have stated that if Palestinian resistance is not crushed in six months, Israel will become another Viet Nam. With this in mind, the United States, England, and the Federal Republic of Germany are presently sending, urgently and frantically, large amounts of weapons to Israel; hundreds of tanks, planes and other technical equipment to help Israel prepare a new aggression against the Arabs. This is quite understandable since Israel is the imperialist base that serves the interests of these powers in that region.

In order to face any new Israeli aggression, the Palestinians have reorganized their ranks. On February 1969, a meeting of the Palestinian National Council took place in Cairo. The result of the meeting was the unification of the various Palestinian organizations: the Liberation Organization, Al Fatah, the Vanguard of the People's War of Liberation, El Saika. They have formed a new Executive Committee for the Organization of Palestinian Liberation. Yasser Arafat, a major of the Al Fatah, was elected head of the Committee with three other members of that organization as members of the 11-member committee.

These new members are very important to the intensification of the Palestinian armed struggle and the strengthening of the militant capacity of the Palestinians to face Israeli aggressions.

Since then, the Palestinian commandos have carried out widespread operations . . .

. . .

While Israel at present concentrates all its troops along the Suez Canal, in Golan, and all along the River Jordan in preparation for the launching of a new aggression aimed at liquidating the Palestinian armed struggle and the camps of the Palestinian commandos, while Israel waits for Washington's authorization to carry out its new plans of aggression, the Palestinian commandos continue to intensify their just armed struggle against the Zionist occupation, with the support of the Arab revolutionaries and of all the revolutionary people of the world.

At the same time, the forces of the Arab countries are in a state of alert to support the Palestinian struggle and to face any new aggression.

The Palestinian armed struggle has confirmed, with its heroic combats, that it is capable of resisting the Zionist aggression. It has also proven to the entire world that the only possible solution is the armed struggle, that it can free Palestine and guarantee the return of two million Palestinian refugees to their country. We are sure that the imperialist plots will be frustrated just as we are sure that the final victory will be the Palestinian people's.

To accept the "peaceful solution" is tantamount to accepting occupation and submitting to the imperialist and Zionist forces in the region.

The real solution proposed by the leaders of the Palestinian armed struggle, Al Fatah, Al Saika, PFPL and all the Arab revolutionaries, is the road taken by the heroic Vietnamese people in their struggle against U.S. imperialism.

It is the true road to liberation, the road of the armed struggle without quarter against imperialism.

The Palestinian people's struggle for liberation forms part of the struggle for world liberation. This struggle is based on the revolutionary forces, within the Palestinian people and the Arab nation, and is waged in collaboration with all the revolutionaries of the world.

The common enemy is U.S. imperialism, ally of the racist Zionist invader of the Middle East.

TERROR IN THE UNITED STATES: "AN INTRODUCTION TO ELEMENTARY TACTICS" AND "SOME QUESTIONS ON TACTICS" 4

by George Prosser

During the second half of the sixties a substantial number of American cities and college campuses were disrupted by riots. The underlying cause for the city disturbances was the explosive pitch of black Americans, impatient with second-class citizenship and now seeking equal rights and opportunities. Dissension over the war in Viet Nam was a major cause of the campus riots, although there were other causes as well, not the least of them the rights issue and a feeling by many students that their studies were not relevant to their needs in the modern world.

The American democracy is a well-meaning system and state of mind, and in the sixties it was not prepared to cope with mass violence. City police departments were neither trained nor equipped to handle major riots. College officials often displayed weakness in the face of the student onslaught. For a while it was the day of the extremist. Any radical shouting on a street corner was sure to receive nationwide news coverage. A black moderate commented ruefully that militant Stokely Carmichael's following "amounts to about fifty Negroes and about 5,000 white reporters."[1]

The American democracy has, however, immeasurable strength, not the least of this being the capacity to make changes when change is genuinely needed. The equal rights movement made its greatest advances since the Emancipation Proclamation, advances in all phases of American life. The Viet Nam issue was largely defused when the new administration of Richard Nixon reversed U.S. policy by carrying out a phased withdrawal of American forces from the war, with a buildup of South Vietnamese forces substituting for American participation.

Dissension over the war and the thrust for civil rights had caused violence, and this violence was frequently magnified by news and broadcast coverage. The vast majority of Americans—even the majority of college students—did not participate in the disturbances. It was this majority that asserted itself, providing justice to the blacks, a wiser policy in Viet Nam—and stronger police departments. Police forces were trained and equipped to prevent riots, and to suppress them if they did occur.

Many militant blacks and youths settled down to work within the established system. Others, however, having tasted violence and liked it, now switched to terrorist activities. A number of extremist groups appeared on the political scene, among them the Black Panthers and the Students for a Democratic Society. Although these organizations professed to be continuing the struggle for rights, it was clear for the most part that their ideological leanings were toward communism.

Bombings and attacks on police officers became the characteristic tactics of the terrorist groups. The Permanent Subcommittee on Investigations of the U.S. Senate's Committee on Government Operations reported that there had been at least 298 explosive bombing and 243 incendiary bombing incidents during 1969. During the first seven months of 1970 there were 301 explosive and 210 incendiary bombing incidents. During the years 1968 and 1969 and the first half of 1970 there were 216 ambushes and snipings against law enforcement officials and facilities. During this period there were a total of 359 assaults of all kinds against police, including bombing attacks, and these assaults resulted in 23 deaths of police officers and 326 injuries to police.[2]

Concurrent with the terrorist acts there was a proliferation of so-called "underground" publications (actually they were sold and circulated quite openly). Uniformly critical of The Establishment, the mood and content of these publications ranged from satire to obscenity, from drug-use discussion to calls for violence and the overthrow of the U.S. government. There were articles on urban warfare and diagrammatical instructions on the making of bombs. Suggestions were somewhat ingenious (construction of a shotgun from a piece of pipe; use of a common cigarette as a time-delay igniter for the fuse of a bomb) and sometimes ludicrous. Note the following suggestion from the *Radical Guide to the University of Maryland*:

> Another idea . . . is to manufacture blow guns. The blow guns . . . can be made from bamboo poles that have been hollowed out. If the jungle isn't near enough and you can't find any bamboo, try a piece of aluminum pipe or tube, or use your head and find something else. The darts for the blow gun can be made from toothpicks with regular pins attached to them with a fine grade of wire. For stability in flight a small feather or piece of paper can be attached to the end of the toothpick. The pin can be dipped into a liquid solution of LSD. . . . The psychological effect on the pigs [police] would indeed be interesting to see. It would probably take only one or two successful shots to make the pigs run at the sight of our blow guns. If there are no pigs around, we could shoot each other.[3]

There follow excerpts from two articles by George Prosser which appeared in *Black Politics*, a Berkeley, California, publication. Prosser, according to the Senate's Permanent Subcommittee on Investigations, is the pen name of Thomas W. Sanders, business manager and editorial board member of *Black Politics* and onetime executive secretary of the pro-Castro Bay Area Fair Play for Cuba Committee.[4] In the first article, Prosser-Sanders sets forth techniques of urban guerrilla warfare. He stresses, as have other guerrilla specialists before him, the need for "correct political education," without which guerrilla activities would be only "uncoordinated, dispersed and risky actions." In the second article, Prosser-Sanders discusses sabotage techniques. The article is a valuable example of the militant viewpoint which sees the United States as highly vulnerable to acts of sabotage and terrorism. There is a clear warning here for all police and security organizations responsible for protecting vital installations and communication and transportation lines in this country.

AN INTRODUCTION TO ELEMENTARY TACTICS
(Excerpts)

The time has come for us to consider some of the elementary tactical principles involved in urban guerrilla warfare, but it should be understood at the outset that we do not advise action *now* to carry out these principles. A certain period of preparation is necessary before armed actions can seriously be considered. Weapons, ammunition, explosives, and much related equipment must be obtained and stockpiled; the terrain must be thoroughly and minutely scrutinized; suitable recruits having the desired revolutionary orientation must be selected and trained; leadership cadres must be formed and given intensive indoctrination and training in revolutionary objectives and methods of struggle; the exceedingly delicate task of building an underground fighting organization must be undertaken at the same time that practical political work is carried out in the ghetto to prepare the masses for resistance. Premature action, whether induced by agents provocateurs in the hire of the police or by well intended but rash and immature individuals, can have but one and the same result—disaster. The period when the forces of resistance are forming and activating their organization is the time of greatest danger. Never again will the organization be so vulnerable to penetration and disruption.

Preparation for armed action without correct political education will only lead to a series of uncoordinated, dispersed, and risky actions in which vital cadres will be wasted; political education without preparations for armed action only leads to the futility of endless meetings, demonstrations, attempts at "pressure" tactics on the existing power structure, and the enervating impotence of the prolonged debating society. Today revolutionary action means ultimately armed action, but before we are ready for that we must become serious students of arms and tactics.

In the previous articles in this journal we have sought to alert our devoted readers to the necessity of acquiring good rifles and ammunition while it was still possible to do so. Now a federal law has been passed which greatly restricts our access to these vital tools (as was predicted by this journal). They are still obtainable, but now only at greater trouble and expense. It is hoped that many of our readers paid heed to our timely advice and have already acquired their weapons and ammunition. Riflemen are made not born. Every fighter has the duty to get himself out to the range while this can still be done and to fire many rounds in practice, preferably under competent supervision from comrades. It is the duty of every group leader to encourage this practice upon the part of his men and to closely supervise this necessary activity. It takes time to train a sharpshooter and *now* is the time for it. Remember that the enemy has a virtually unlimited supply of ammunition and his great volumes of fire can only be effectively countered by accurate, *aimed* fire. Unless you can make consistent hits on a target the size of a man's head at one hundred yards, a target which moreover will probably be bobbing about and only visible for brief intervals, you are not good enough.

After mastering the technique of aimed fire both in daylight and darkness, we must study the fundamentals of tactics so that we shall learn how to apply these principles in actual battle situations. Correct tactics are difficult to learn, and a certain theoretical knowledge is necessary. The trouble with learning tactics through actual experience, i.e., "learning by doing," is that mistakes can have serious, even fatal, consequences. We must start thinking about these problems, asking questions and seeking answers, and we must carefully study and analyze every action that has taken place so far, especially those that had unforseen and undesired results, in order that we might learn from these experiences.

Exposure and Cover

The most fundamental principle with respect to warfare in the cities concerns *exposure* and *cover*.

Exposure means being exposed to enemy fire without being in a good position to return it; cover means being in a position where you have reasonable protection from enemy fire while at the same time being able to return it effectively. Being exposed to enemy fire while still being able to return it is serious, but you are not too badly off; after all, your fire may succeed in suppressing the enemy fire. Being in cover but without being able to return the fire is always disastrous. It is just as bad as being completely exposed; it will only be a matter of time, and a short time, until the enemy closes in on you and completes the kill.

It follows that we must be seriously concerned with the problems of exposure and cover, and with concealed fire positions, in any consideration of the nature of urban guerrilla warfare. According to Captain S. J. Cuthbert, an authority on street fighting, there are three fundamental principles with respect to this form of warfare which must be thoroughly understood and digested:

1. No other type of terrain is either so open or so close. In every street there are coverless stretches, ideal fields of fire, deathtraps to the unwary attackers. Bordering every street are a hundred protected firing positions, a hundred hiding places, a hundred possible ambush positions.
2. It is possible to climb 30, 50, perhaps 100 feet in as many seconds. Street fighting thus possesses a third dimension, not often present in field warfare.
3. Cities present exceptionally blind and disjointed conditions. In no other form of warfare are there such narrow horizons, or such ruthless divisions between units of the same force.

He concludes by reasserting the principle rule with regard to street warfare: USE COVER. NEVER HANG ABOUT IN THE OPEN!

This expert military advice, given by one who is a serious student of the problem, is something that we should ponder well. We should try to apply these principles to the conditions of fighting that we expect to encounter. Let us see what some of these considerations are.

First, we shall never be able to match the enemy in sheer volume of fire. We must expect that he will always have an advantage in this regard. He will easily be able to transform any open stretch of street into a deathtrap for anything that moves. But this should not make us pessimistic, because the very nature of urban terrain provides us with a countervailing advantage, namely, we shall have numberless covered positions, in close proximity to the open streets, from which we can direct concealed fire against the enemy. It is almost impossible to be more than a few yards from cover at any time.

Knowledge of the Terrain

This leads us then to another very important principle, namely, *know your terrain*. When the enemy invades our areas in force, he will for the most part be confined to the streets. His heavy vehicles will be a disadvantage for him in this respect. He will present an appearance of imposing power, but unless you are so considerate as to place yourself directly in his path, he will find it difficult to bring his power to bear. He will dominate the streets, the open stretches, but everything beyond his limited horizons, everything behind the houses, between the houses, and in the houses will be terra incognita to him. It follows that we must become intensively familiar with our own terrain. *It is the principal advantage we have over the enemy*.

For the revolutionary fighter, there can be no excuse for not mastering, in every detail, the terrain over which he expects to fight. With respect to this important task, no complacency can be tolerated. Group leaders must instruct their units in this important principle, and intensive and thorough examinations of the terrain must be conducted in an organized way until every member of the group is thoroughly acquainted with it. The leadership must take this responsibility; it cannot be left to individual initiative!

You must examine the terrain foot by foot. You must memorize every alley, every underpass, every house and building, taking especial note of all cover and of all routes of movement and escape. On one pretext or another you must gain access to all of the back alleys and gardens, you must cross the fences, you must learn the routes through these areas. You must take careful note of all possible places of concealment, places of movement, places of ambush. This is your terrain; this is where you will fight.

Above all, you must learn and remember every *cul de sac*. Cul de sac is a military term borrowed from the French language. It means a pocket or enclosed place from which there is no escape. Such places will be deathtraps during the fighting; you must learn where they are and avoid them so that you will not mistakenly flee into one of them after completing a mission or while being pursued by a counterattacking force.

Backyards and gardens provide good concealment from view while also providing serious obstacles to attack or pursuit. Thorough familiarity with this terrain is one of the major advantages you will have over the enemy. Not everybody who lives in a neighborhood all his life will have this familiarity with the terrain. Human beings are creatures of habit, like most living things, and they tend to stick to well defined paths. Ask yourself the questions, "Do you really know what is behind that row of houses across the street? Would you be able to maneuver through it, quickly and surely, if you had to?" If the answer is "No," better get over there and take a look.

Mobility

Another very important principle is that of mobility. Again, this principle relates directly to the superiority of conventional means of firepower enjoyed by the enemy. Because of this fire superiority, you must never allow yourself to be pinned down, to lose mobility. For that reason, it is usually suicide to hole up in a house. Most houses are not suitable for protracted defense, unless heavily reinforced. They can easily be riddled with bullets from the .50 calibre machine run mounted on an ordinary weapons carrier, or blown apart by the gun mounted on a light tank. The only way they can be successfully defended is by constructing reinforced machine gun nests at the corners of the basement, at ground level. Even so, as soon as encirclement is completed, it is only a matter of time until the defenders are smoked out and destroyed. The rule to remember is: do not hole up in a house and stay there long enough for the enemy to complete an encirclement. If pursued, it is alright to take cover in a house temporarily, just long enough to delay the enemy, and force him to take cover, with a few well-aimed shots. Then, get on through the house and out the back of it, and move on. Maneuver into another firing position from which to direct fire at the enemy and again move on. The guerrilla fighting in urban terrain must move about like quicksilver. (It goes without saying, never erect barricades.)

Fighting at Night

A very important aspect of cover is darkness. In fact, most of your fighting will be done under cover of darkness. It is essential, therefore, that you know your terrain well enough to be able to maneuver through it quickly and surely at night, and that you know how to fire your weapons accurately at night. Weapons suitable for use at night are the rifle, submachine gun, automatic shotgun loaded with the heaviest buckshot, and hand grenades. A certain kind of telescopic sight, with low magnification but high luminosity, can be mounted on a rifle and aids greatly in the location and identification of targets in dim light. Among the essential weapons that should be carried by each squad are a strong axe, preferably of the "fireman" type, and a heavy crowbar. These can be used to break through the walls of houses, creating passages through which soldiers can move without exposing themselves in the streets. Gas masks are also essential for protection against toxic agents.

•   •   •

Before concluding this initial consideration of some of the principles of elementary tactics it is desirable to mention the greatest danger that any resistance organization ever faces in its entire career. This is the danger of exposure and destruction by enemy intelligence agents, especially during the *early* stages of the formation of the resistance groups. During these early stages, when the groups are in the process of acquiring adherents, when lines of communication are being established, when weapons and ammunition are being acquired and stockpiled, when loyal and suspect members are being evaluated and screened, in short, during the period of initial organization and activation, this is when you will be most vulnerable to penetration by enemy agents. The oppressor government employs these agents in huge numbers, and it is safe to say that our areas are saturated with them. These agents and informers must be neutralized without mercy whenever there is any possibility whatever that they will penetrate an organization and give away its secrets. At no later time, not even during the most critical situations of pursuit or encirclement, will the resistance forces be so vulnerable. It follows that during these initial stages nothing should ever be done deliberately to provoke the enemy or give him an excuse for retaliation.

. . .

SOME QUESTIONS ON TACTICS (Excerpts)

Since electoral politics has failed, since peace marching has failed, since writing letters to congressmen has failed, since the whole apparatus of bourgeois parliamentary democracy has failed, what, then, is to be done? I am sure that a great many people are thinking in terms of direct action. They are thinking of how to derail the train.

A discussion of this question is of great importance to anyone interested in doing something to force our criminal government to bring its war of atrocity to an end. And force is what will have to be used, because you do not appeal to the sentiments of an international gangster. A great many people have already recognized this fact, and are groping toward a solution. It is a safe prediction, therefore, that such actions will take place with increasing frequency as the endless war in Asia continues to take its toll and as the bitterness and frustrations of the impoverished millions at home, in particular the ghetto dwellers vents itself in outbursts of violence. As serious students of the military and political trends of our time, our only question is, what form will this direct action take? The question is not entirely academic. The answers may have an important bearing on our lives.

My prediction is that direct action will take two forms, terrorism and sabotage. Without in any sense advocating either of these forms of action, it nevertheless seems useful to examine them, to attempt at least a rough projection of what they will look like, and to assess the probable results.

·   ·   ·

The United States certainly presents a picture of formidable power, both military and economic. It is the most powerful beast in the jungle. On the surface, it appears invincible. Yet this appearance may be illusory. The world's mightiest war machine, employed with a complete disregard for all of the civilized norms, carrying on virtually unrestricted and indiscriminate warfare without regard for any distinction between soldier and civilian, has been unable to defeat the Vietnamese people. That is certainly a tribute to the brave Vietnamese, but it also suggests that there are limits to the application of the kind of military power that the United States has at its disposal. The significant question for us is, is the military machine vulnerable at home?

Any serious consideration of this question must commence with another, namely, *why should the U.S. military be allowed the privilege, unprecedented in the history of warfare, of a long, vulnerable and virtu-*

ally unprotected supply line? It is a question to ponder. Just think of what it would mean if the government had to deploy troops to guard that supply line? Where would they get them? Either they would have to increase the draft calls, at a time when resistance to the draft is increasing at a geometric rate, or they would have to call up the reserves, which would be politically very unpopular. The only other alternative would be to withdraw troops from Vietnam, at a time when the U.S. Command in Vietnam can barely hold onto its bases and infrastructure under continuing offensives by the N.L.F. Forcing the government to withdraw troops from Vietnam would be a victory, of course.

We here are sitting right next to that vital supply line, because it passes through the San Francisco Bay area. So are the people sitting in Chicago, because all of the country's major railroad lines converge there. It is a potential bottleneck, a narrow isthmus of transport which, if pinched off, would bring the whole system to a halt. Even without organized sabotage, there have already occurred severe difficulties and bottlenecks, resulting in serious shortages of munitions and supplies in the fighting zone. It must be remembered that to fight the kind of war the U.S. is fighting in Vietnam requires astronomical quantities of ammunition. It has only been through the expenditure of an enormous quantity of firepower that the U.S. has held the N.L.F. at bay. Only a vastly wealthy country could afford such a prodigal waste. The ammunition cannot be expended, of course, if it does not reach its destination, and reach it on time to be of tactical value. In general, it is quite proper to point out that the powerful American military industrial machine, precisely because it is so sophisticated and because its many complex parts are so interrelated, is extremely vulnerable to disruption. I do not think that the domestic opposition to the war has thought very seriously about this; I know that the planners in Washington have thought about it. Indeed, I am quite sure that the prospects are giving some of them nightmares. Sometimes paranoids do have real enemies.

The second proposition to be pondered is that munitions are highly explosive. Continuing our scenario, we should ask ourselves why those munitions should wait until they get all the way to Vietnam before they are exploded. They are laying about here in immense dumps which constitute unprecedented concentrations of explosive power. If they were set off, the havoc wrought would be considerable, and very little would be required to set them off. An entire ammunition dump can be set off by one 81-millimeter mortar shell dropped into the right place. A mortar is a very simple, cheap weapon, and it can be operated by a crew of three men. Allow another half dozen, armed with rifles, as guards for the

mortar teams, and you have less than a standard army squad, a tactical
unit capable of destroying Port Chicago entirely and leveling most of
the adjacent countryside. Surely that is a degree of military efficiency
not contemplated in the textbooks. Just reflect upon what one N.L.F.
mortar team did to the great American airbase at Pleiku. They wrought
about five billion dollars worth of damage. And they did it after successfully penetrating an elaborate network of defense facilities. There are no
elaborate defensive networks surrounding American supply dumps and
port facilities in the continental U.S.A. The military authorities are
aware of the passivity and docility of the American people, and the self-
inflicted castration of the pacifists who have attempted feebly to disrupt
the supply lines with ineffectual nonviolent demonstrations. The authorities have not deployed the troops to set up secure defense perimeters.
They don't want to do so, either; it would remove too many combat
troops from the frontlines in Vietnam, where they are desperately
needed

The Navy has long been aware of the extreme vulnerability of their
gigantic weapons depot at Port Chicago; for this reason they have clam-
ored for legislation to enable them to buy up the whole town of Port
Chicago. This is now being done. The alleged reason, given out in the
form of soothing public relations syrup, is to "protect" all of those innocent civilians in the event of an accidental explosion. This sudden con-
version to humanitarianism on the part of professional killers would be
amusing if it were not ludicrous. The real reason, of course, is to enable
them to extend the defense perimeter. Thus far they have shown more
imagination than their opponents in the antiwar movement.

Not only is Port Chicago laden with an enormous concentration of
explosives. (Eighty percent of the munitions used in Vietnam pass
through there.) But it is also laden with inflammables. A great explosion
would be likely to result in a great fire. Such an event would certainly
impede the flow of munitions to Vietnam for a long time. There is no
question that it would severely impair the American war effort there.

Suppose the Unexpected Should Happen

Think of the impact one such event would have on the planners
in Washington. Think of what it would do to them if they knew that
they had to cope with a *serious* domestic opposition, and not a theatri-
cal one. For that matter, think of what it would mean to the longshore-
men who load those munitions into ships bound for Vietnam. Thus far

those noble proletarians have been quite content to draw their not insub-
stantial wages, $15,000-$20,000 a year in most cases, for loading cargoes
of death for Vietnamese with very little trouble from their consciences.
After all, as everyone knows, all that really counts is the dollar. They are
as sunken in degeneracy and vice as the majority of their fellow-country-
men; they are as ready to swill greedily at the bloody trough as any
swollen bourgeois. The only complaint heard out of them for a long
time is that they aren't getting enough. I say that it would make quite a
difference if they were suddenly made to realize that theirs is a dangerous trade. The prospect of a Vietnamese mother or child being incinerated alive by napalm or white phosphorous may not touch them very
deeply; but the prospect of their own precious hides being roasted would
surely cause them to pause and reflect. Suddenly they might begin to remember their consciences, perhaps.

. . .

According to the most recent information I have all of the napalm
being used in Vietnam is being manufactured in Torrance, California, a
town just outside of Long Beach. That must be a very inflammable place.
Also, it is fairly close to a lot of oil wells. That is natural enough, since
napalm is made from refined petroleum. That one plant is efficient
enough to produce all of the napalm needed to roast Vietnamese. It
would burn just as efficiently in Torrance as in Vietnam, it goes without
saying.

In one small town in the East, in Connecticut or New Hampshire, I
believe, is a factory which is manufacturing all of the helicopters being
used in Vietnam. Helicopters are vitally necessary to the kind of war the
United States is waging.

The communications network is vulnerable to disruption. So is the
power grid. So are roads and bridges. Modern aircraft, with their complex electronic equipment, are easily destroyed. There are great airfields, jammed with expensive military aircraft, lying unprotected all
over the country.

. . .

Let us cite a few . . . examples of the simplicity and effectiveness of
techniques of sabotage. One man crawling into the cab of a diesel locomotive, with no weapon other than a sledge hammer, can wreak havoc
with a multi-billion dollar piece of machinery in five minutes by destroying the instrument panel.

To sabotage railroad lines requires only the simplest equipment, crow-
bars and sledge hammers. To derail a train all that is necessary is to loosen
the tie mounting on eight successive ties. Remove the fishplate and ap-

ply leverage with a crowbar so as to move one rail toward the inside. Jam the fishplate in between.

In all likelihood that is the technique that was used by the enterprising saboteurs who derailed the 40-car S. P. freight train near Fairfield on the 20th of March. Six of the cars caught fire. According to another newspaper report, they also loosened enough ties so that the tracks simply spread apart under the weight of the locomotive.

Tossing a hand grenade or a charge of explosive into the air intake of a jet engine will destroy the aircraft.

Throwing a handful of sand, abrasive powder, or metal shavings into the grease boxes on rolling stock will ruin the bearings. Grease boxes on freight cars can easily be opened. No immediate results will be seen, but the eventual damage will be considerable.

Greasing railroad tracks on inclines with heavy grease, oil, soft soap, et cetera, will block the stretch.

Merely knocking off the screw heads holding the rails to the track is effective. If this sabotage does not derail a train, it will at least keep the maintenance engineers busy.

Shooting out the insulators on high tension power lines with a small bore rifle fitted with a telescopic sight will seriously damage the line. If the insulators are shot so that the power line falls down onto the support structure, it will short-circuit and melt the line. Indeed, the principal aim of all sabotage of electrical power grids should be to short-circuit the system.

To severely damage high-tension lines, if no explosives with which to destroy the tower are available, it is only necessary to establish connection with the ground. Attach a heavy wire or light cable to a metal fence post or a metal stake driven about five feet into the ground. Attach a heavy piece of metal to the other end of the cable, and throw it over the line. If the saboteur does not release the cable as soon as it is thrown, he may be electrocuted.

In the past few years giant computers have become vital to every large industrial corporation, research center, university, military and police headquarters, and many government operations. Computers are expensive, delicate mechanisms. They are vulnerable to sabotage. If a five gallon can of gasoline with a small explosive charge taped to it is placed in a room close to a computer, the resulting explosion and fire will destroy not only the computer but all the tapes and records as well. For such operations a standard blasting cap and length of fuse should always be used. Timing devices are notoriously unreliable and dangerous to the user.

All modern institutions depend heavily upon records. Pay records, scholastic records, research papers, priceless blueprints, industrial secrets —all are printed on paper. (Not all these records are duplicated on microfilm and stored in vaults.) Documents are easily incinerated.

If sugar is put into the gas tanks of motor vehicles, the sabotage cannot be detected, and as soon as the vehicle is driven the engine will be totally ruined. Another method of sabotage is simply to cut part way through a hydraulic brake line with an ordinary wire cutter until a slow leak starts, then loosen the emergency brake cable if there is time.

These are just a few examples of some very simple techniques. If you use your imagination, no doubt you could think of many more. Such techniques are not to be despised. If practiced by a great number of individuals, in a great number of places, they could effectively hamper the industrial war effort and drive the authorities wild. Their principal advantage is that no great skill is required, nor hard-to-get weapons. They can be accomplished by relatively small, tightly knit groups; or even in some cases by lone individuals. Human casualties are avoided, except as a result of accident. There is a plethora of targets.

It is only necessary for an attacking force, small in number, to strike at a railroad network a few times in separate places, *and the authorities will be forced to defend all of it*, at great cost. Such is the efficiency of guerrilla methods of warfare. Consider one well-known example of this method in the Balkans during World War II. Tito's partisans never numbered more than about 3,000 men at their peak; the average was about 1,000. Yet this relatively small force held down twelve German divisions which were badly needed elsewhere.

More effective sabotage can be done if explosives are available. With them high-tension towers can be knocked down, preferably in such a manner that the tower carrying the lines falls into a relay station or into other lines. Bridges can be blasted, blocking waterways and impeding road or rail traffic. Water mains and pumping stations can be attacked, so that water pressure is reduced, preventing the suppression of fires. With still heavier weapons, such as mortars and machine guns, ammo depots and napalm storage dumps can be attacked.

At its Dugway Proving Grounds in Utah for chemical and biological weapons the army maintains huge storage tanks filled with lethal nerve gas above ground and unprotected except for a handful of security guards. (The gas is now being transported to a site near Salt Lake City.) To adequately guard those tanks would require a regiment of marines; the government does not have regiments of marines to guard every vulnerable storage depot in the country. Nerve gas is transported in tank trucks over lonely roads. In the event of an accident, prevailing winds would carry that gas to population centers.

The government has been spending huge sums of money in its program to put a man on the moon, while neglecting important areas of social need affecting millions of our citizens. Even now, desperately needed social programs are being ruthlessly cut back as an economy measure. A moon rocket is a flying bomb, loaded with highly explosive fuel. It is a huge target. A single .30 caliber machine gun, with tracer ammunition, placed a thousand yards away with a competent gunner behind it, can blow up the Saturn lunar rocket on its pad. How would that look on TV? Who knows, perhaps someone has already thought of it.

·   ·   ·

A most important aspect of any campaign of sabotage is psychological warfare. Is is essential that the people know that sabotage is being done, and why. Every act of sabotage, therefore, should be immediately followed by a communique from the underground headquarters, distributed by handbills, leaflets, underground press or radio, describing the act of sabotage and relating it to the struggle against the war, against imperialist intervention, against racism, and so forth. This also prevents the authorities from covering up events, from depicting sabotage as accidents or the work of disturbed persons, et cetera. This psychological impact of sabotage is so important that it can be said that any group which neglects it is throwing away half the battle.

·   ·   ·

MINIMANUAL OF THE URBAN GUERRILLA 5

by Carlos Marighella

The Cuban Revolution, launched in 1956, included terrorism as one aspect of the struggle. Terrorism was not a new form of warfare on the Latin American scene: Cubans and Latin Americans in general were already familiar with bombings and assassinations carried out by clandestine political organizations.

The revolution in Cuba took place basically within two spheres of conflict. In the hills were the guerrillas; in the cities and towns, the underground fighters. The guerrillas, in their fastnesses, were more isolated than the urban fighters, who were involved in a daily and deadly struggle with the police. The situation was far more dangerous for the clandestine organizations that operated within the government's city citadels, and several underground leaders who might have challenged Fidel Castro in authority and stature died under police gunfire. Favoring the guerrillas was the fact that they had Castro, a charismatic individual who conquered the romantic imaginations of much of the country's citizenry.

Once the rebel victory had placed Castro in power, the cultivation of a guerrilla mystique was started. It suited Castro's ego that he be viewed historically as a great military leader. It also suited his political situation at the time, for if he and his guerrillas were credited with the rebel triumph, this placed them in a better position in the post-victory struggle for control of Cuba.

Virtually ignoring the decisive role of the underground in the revolution, Castro and Ernesto Guevara talked so much about the supposed guerrilla victory that they came to believe in it. When they began planning to export revolution to other countries, guerrilla warfare was their chosen instrument. Guevara declared that "guerrilla action . . . [is to be the] central axis of the struggle."[1]

A number of Cuban-sponsored guerrilla operations were launched in Latin American countries. Although one or two grew to dangerous proportions, none succeeded in overthrowing established governments. The governments and the military had learned from the Cuban example, and with United States assistance and advice, were able to contain, and eventually in most cases, to destroy the guerrilla units. Urban warfare was also waged by revolutionaries, but in the Cuban view guerrilla fighting was of paramount importance. In a speech on 13 March 1967 Castro faulted Venezuelan revolutionaries because there had been in their strategy "an over-estimation of the importance of the capital and of the struggle in the capital and an under-estimation of the importance of the guerrilla movement."[2]

Even as Castro was making this statement, Guevara was in Bolivia, preparing to launch a guerrilla operation in that country. The Guevara movement was to form part of a pincers. The other prong was to be in Venezuela, where two additional high-ranking officials of the Cuban government and army, Raúl Menéndez Tomassevich and Orestes Guerra González, also attempted to shape a guerrilla movement. Guevara failed and died; Tomassevich and Guerra failed but made it back to Cuba.

With the collapse of the grand design for guerrilla conquest, Latin American revolutionaries turned toward increased urban warfare, and particularly terror tactics. A leading proponent of this type of activity was a Brazilian, Carlos Marighella. Born in Salvador, Brazil on 5 December 1911 of a middle-class family, Marighella became a Communist militant by his mid-teens, and at the age of 20 he left engineering school to join an organization that provided refuge for Communists on the run from the police. He may have participated in a Communist uprising which occurred in 1935.

The following year Marighella was arrested for distributing Communist pamphlets and spent a year in jail. He was arrested twice more in the succeeding years and was subjected to tortures in prison. Following the fall of the Getulio Vargas regime in 1945, Marighella ran on the Communist ticket and won a seat in the Federal Chamber of Deputies. The Communist party was again outlawed in 1947. Marighella traveled extensively in Communist countries, but at home his activities were largely clandestine. In 1964 he was again arrested but was released a few months later.

Marighella rejected Moscow's *vía pacífica* policy toward Latin

America. He attended the Latin American Organization of Solidarity conference held in Havana in 1967. The conference was aimed at expanding Castroite subversion in the hemisphere. When he returned to Brazil, Marighella was expelled from the Moscow-line Brazilian Communist party. He set up his own extremist organization, calling it the *Ala Marighella* (Marighella Wing), and later organized a loose coalition of urban terror groups. The *Minimanual of the Urban Guerrilla*, written by Carlos Marighella, became the operational handbook for these groups.

The end came for Marighella on 4 November 1969. He was caught in a police trap in the city of São Paulo and killed. Two days later he was buried in a pauper's grave.

The *Minimanual* was written specifically for Brazil, but its contents are clearly applicable elsewhere as well. It provides precise instructions on the conduct of various types of urban warfare, including terrorism, of which Marighella says, "Terrorism is an arm the revolutionary can never relinquish." In Marighella's view, "To be an assailant or a terrorist ennobles any honorable man."

So modern is the manual that it mentions the hijacking of airplanes as one of the courses of action open to urban guerrillas. The kidnapping of certain individuals, including well-known personalities, is also advocated by Marighella. He states that kidnapping can be used as a method "to exchange or liberate imprisoned revolutionary comrades," and this technique has now come to the fore as one of the principal weapons utilized by Latin American terrorists. (It has been attempted in Canada, and there is a danger that some day it may be used by terrorists in the United States.)

Ernesto Guevara was an activist and a writer-theoretician. Marighella was an activist and a writer-theoretician. Marighella, operating in dark clandestineness, never achieved nearly as much fame as Guevara. Because of his *Minimanual*, however, he may well become known as the Guevara of urban warfare.

MINIMANUAL OF THE URBAN GUERRILLA

By Way of Introduction

I would like to make a twofold dedication of this work: first to the memories of Edson Souto, Marco Antonio Brás de Carvalho, Nelson José de Almeida ("Escoteiro"), and so many of the heroic fighters and urban guerrillas who fell at the hands of assassins of the Military Police, the Army, the Navy, the Air Force, and the DOPS,[3] hated instruments of the repressive military dictatorship.

Second, to the brave comrades—men and women—imprisoned in the medieval dungeons of the Brazilian government and subjected to tortures that even surpass the horrendous crimes practiced by the Nazis.

Like those comrades whose memory we revere, as well as those taken prisoner in battle, what we must do is fight.

Each comrade who opposes the military dictatorship and wants to fight it can do something, however insignificant the task may seem.

I urge all who read this minimanual and reach the conclusion that they cannot remain inactive, to follow its instructions and join the fight now. I do so because, under whatever hypothesis and in whatever circumstances, the duty of every revolutionary is to make the revolution.

Another important problem is not merely to read the minimanual here and now, but to circulate its contents. This circulation will be possible if those who agree with its ideas make mimeographed copies or print it in a pamphlet, though in this latter case, armed struggle itself will be necessary.

Finally, the reason that the present minimanual bears my signature, is that the ideas expressed or systematized here reflect the personal experience of a group of men engaged in armed struggle in Brazil, among whom I have the honor to be included. So that certain individuals will have no doubt about what this minimanual proclaims and can no longer deny the facts or continue to state that the conditions for the struggle do not exist, it is necessary to assume responsibility for what is said and done. Hence anonymity becomes a problem in a work such as this. The important fact is that there are patriots prepared to fight like ordinary soldiers, and the more there are the better.

The accusation of assault or terrorism no longer has the pejorative meaning it used to have. It has acquired new clothing, a new coloration. It does not factionalize, it does not discredit; on the contrary it represents a focal point of attraction.

Today to be an assailant or a terrorist is a quality that ennobles any honorable man because it is an act worthy of a revolutionary engaged in armed struggle against the shameful military dictatorship and its monstrosities.

A Definition of the Urban Guerrilla

The chronic structural crisis characteristic of Brazil today, and its resultant political instability, are what have brought about the upsurge of revolutionary war in the country. The revolutionary war manifests itself in the form of urban guerrilla warfare, psychological warfare, or rural guerrilla warfare. Urban guerrilla warfare or psychological warfare in the city depends on the urban guerrilla.

The urban guerrilla is a man who fights the military dictatorship with arms, using unconventional methods. A political revolutionary and an ardent patriot, he is a fighter for his country's liberation, a friend of the people and of freedom. The area in which the urban guerrilla acts is in the large Brazilian cities. There are also bandits, commonly known as outlaws, who work in the big cities. Many times assaults by outlaws are taken as actions by urban guerrillas.

The urban guerrilla, however, differs radically from the outlaw. The outlaw benefits personally from the action, and attacks indiscriminately without distinguishing between the exploited and the exploiters, which is why there are so many ordinary men and women among his victims. The urban guerrilla follows a political goal and only attacks the government, the big capitalists, and the foreign imperialists, particularly North Americans.

Another element just as prejudicial as the outlaw and also operating in the urban area is the right-wing counterrevolutionary who creates confusion, assaults banks, hurls bombs, kidnaps, assassinates, and commits the worst imaginable crimes against urban guerrillas, revolutionary priests, students, and citizens who oppose fascism and seek liberty.

The urban guerrilla is an implacable enemy of the government and systematically inflicts damage on the authorities and on the men who dominate the country and exercise power. The principal task of the urban guerrilla is to distract, to wear out, to demoralize the militarists, the military dictatorship and its repressive forces, and also to attack and destroy the wealth and property of the North Americans, the foreign managers, and the Brazilian upper class.

The urban guerrilla is not afraid of dismantling and destroying the present Brazilian economic, political, and social system, for his aim is to help the rural guerrilla and to collaborate in the creation of a totally new and revolutionary social and political structure, with the armed people in power.

The urban guerrilla must have a certain minimal political understanding. To gain that he must read certain printed or mimeographed works such as:

Guerrilla Warfare by Che Guevara
Memories of a Terrorist
Some Questions about the Brazilian
    Guerrilla Operations and Tactics
On Strategic Problems and Principles
Certain Tactical Principles for Comrades Undertaking
    Guerrilla Operations
Organizational Questions
O Guerrilheiro, newspaper of the Brazilian revolutionary groups.

Personal Qualities of the Urban Guerrilla

The urban guerrilla is characterized by his bravery and decisive nature. He must be a good tactician and a good shot. The urban guerrilla must be a person of great astuteness to compensate for the fact that he is not sufficiently strong in arms, ammunition, and equipment.

The career militarists or the government police have modern arms and transport, and can go about anywhere freely, using the force of their power. The urban guerrilla does not have such resources at his disposal and leads to a clandestine existence. Sometimes he is a convicted person or is out on parole, and is obliged to use false documents.

Nevertheless, the urban guerrilla has a certain advantage over the conventional military or the police. It is that, while the military and the police act on behalf of the enemy, whom the people hate, the urban guerrilla defends a just cause, which is the people's cause.

The urban guerrilla's arms are inferior to the enemy's, but from a moral point of view, the urban guerrilla has an undeniable superiority.

This moral superiority is what sustains the urban guerrilla. Thanks to it, the urban guerrilla can accomplish his principal duty, which is to attack and to survive.

The urban guerrilla has to capture or divert arms from the enemy to be able to fight. Because his arms are not uniform, since what he has are expropriated or have fallen into his hands in different ways, the urban guerrilla faces the problem of a variety of arms and a shortage of ammunition. Moreover, he has no place to practice shooting and marksmanship.

These difficulties have to be surmounted, forcing the urban guerrilla to be imaginative and creative, qualities without which it would be impossible for him to carry out his role as a revolutionary.

The urban guerrilla must possess initiative, mobility, and flexibility, as well as versatility and a command of any situation. Initiative especially is an indispensable quality. It is not always possible to foresee everything , and the urban guerrilla cannot let himself become confused, or wait for orders. His duty is to act, to find adequate solutions for each problem he faces, and not to retreat. It is better to err acting than to do nothing for fear of erring. Without initiative there is no urban guerrilla warfare.

Other important qualities in the urban guerrilla are the following: to be a good walker, to be able to stand up against fatigue, hunger, rain, heat. To know how to hide and to be vigilant. To conquer the art of dissembling. Never to fear danger. To behave the same by day as by night. Not to act impetuously. To have unlimited patience. To remain calm and cool in the worst conditions and situations. Never to leave a track or trail. Not to get discouraged.

In the face of the almost insurmountable difficulties of urban warfare, sometimes comrades weaken, leave, give up the work.

The urban guerrilla is not a businessman in a commercial firm nor is he a character in a play. Urban guerrilla warfare, like rural guerrilla warfare, is a pledge the guerrilla makes to himself. When he cannot face the difficulties, or knows that he lacks the patience to wait, then it is better to relinquish his role before he betrays his pledge, for he clearly lacks the basic qualities necessary to be a guerrilla.

How the Urban Guerrilla Lives and Subsists

The urban guerrilla must know how to live among the people and must be careful not to appear strange and separated from ordinary city life.

He should not wear clothes that are different from those that other people wear. Elaborate and high fashion clothing for men or women may often be a handicap if the urban guerrilla's mission takes him into working class neighborhoods or sections where such dress is uncommon.

The same care has to be taken if the urban guerrilla moves from the South to the North or vice versa.

The urban guerrilla must live by his work or professional activity. If he is known and sought by the police, if he is convicted or is on parole, he must go underground and sometimes must live hidden. Under such circumstances, the urban guerrilla cannot reveal his activity to anyone, since that is always and only the responsibility of the revolutionary organization in which he is participating.

The urban guerrilla must have a great capacity for observation, must be well informed about everything, principally about the enemy's movements, and must be very searching and knowledgeable about the area in which he lives, operates, or through which he moves.

But the fundamental and decisive characteristic of the urban guerrilla is that he is a man who fights with arms; given this condition, there is very little likelihood that he will be able to follow his normal profession for long without being identified. The role of expropriation thus looms as clear as high noon. It is impossible for the urban guerrilla to exist and survive without fighting to expropriate.

Thus, within the framework of the class struggle, as it inevitably and necessarily sharpens, the armed struggle of the urban guerrilla points toward two essential objectives:

    a) the physical liquidation of the chiefs and assistants of the armed forces and of the police;

    b) the expropriation of government resources and those belonging to the big capitalists, latifundists, and imperialists, with small expropriations used for the maintenance of individual urban guerrillas and large ones for the sustenance of the revolution itself.

It is clear that the armed struggle of the urban guerrilla also has other objectives. But here we are referring to the two basic objectives, above all expropriation. It is necessary for every urban guerrilla to keep in mind always that he can only maintain his existence if he is disposed to kill the police and those dedicated to repression, and if he is determined —truly determined—to expropriate the wealth of the big capitalists, the latifundists, and the imperialists.

One of the fundamental characteristics of the Brazilian revolution is that from the beginning it developed around the expropriation of the wealth of the major bourgeois, imperialist, and latifundist interests, without excluding the richest and most powerful commercial elements engaged in the import-export business.

And by expropriating the wealth of the principal enemies of the people, the Brazilian revolution was able to hit them at their vital center, with preferential and systematic attacks on the banking network—that is to say, the most telling blows were leveled against capitalism's nerve system.

The bank robberies carried out by the Brazilian urban guerrillas hurt such big capitalists as Moreira Salles and others, the foreign firms which insure and reinsure the banking capital, the imperialist companies, the federal and state governments—all of them systematically expropriated as of now.

The fruit of these expropriations has been devoted to the work of learning and perfecting urban guerrilla techniques, the purchase, the production, and the transportation of arms and ammunition for the rural areas, the security apparatus of the revolutionaries, the daily maintenance of the fighters, of those who have been liberated from prison by armed force and those who are wounded or persecuted by the police, or to any kind of problem concerning comrades liberated from jail, or assassinated by the police and the military dictatorship.

The tremendous costs of the revolutionary war must fall on the big capitalists, on imperialism, and the latifundists and on the government, too, both federal and state, since they are all exploiters and oppressors of the people.

Men of the government, agents of the dictatorship and of North American imperialism principally, must pay with their lives for the crimes committed against the Brazilian people.

In Brazil, the number of violent actions carried out by urban guerrillas, including deaths, explosions, seizures of arms, ammunition, and explosives, assaults on banks and prisons, etc., is significant enough to leave no room for doubt as to the actual aims of the revolutionaries. The execution of the CIA spy Charles Chandler,[4] a member of the U.S. Army who came from the war in Viet-Nam to infiltrate the Brazilian student movement, the military henchmen killed in bloody encounters with urban guerrillas, all are witness to the fact that we are in full revolutionary war and that the war can be waged only by violent means.

This is the reason why the urban guerrilla uses armed struggle and why he continues to concentrate his activity on the physical extermination of the agents of repression, and to dedicate twenty-four hours a day to expropriation from the people's exploiters.

Technical Preparation of the Urban Guerrilla

No one can become an urban guerrilla without paying special attention to technical preparation.

The technical preparation of the urban guerrilla runs from the concern for his physical preparedness, to knowledge of and apprenticeship in professions and skills of all kinds, particularly manual skills.

The urban guerrilla can have strong physical resistance only if he trains systematically. He cannot be a good fighter if he has not learned the art of fighting. For that reason the urban guerrilla must learn and practice various kinds of fighting, of attack, and personal defense.

Other useful forms of physical preparation are hiking, camping, and practice in survival in the woods, mountain climbing, rowing, swimming, skin diving, training as a frogman, fishing, harpooning, and the hunting of birds, small and big game.

It is very important to learn how to drive, pilot a plane, handle a motor boat and a sail boat, understand mechanics, radio, telephone, electricity, and have some knowledge of electronic techniques.

It is also important to have a knowledge of topographical information, to be able to locate one's position by instruments or other available resources, to calculate distances, make maps and plans, draw to scale, make timings, work with an angle protractor, a compass, etc.

A knowledge of chemistry and of color combination, of stampmaking, the domination of the technique of calligraphy and the copying of letters and other skills are part of the technical preparation of the urban guerrilla, who is obliged to falsify documents in order to live within a society that he seeks to destroy.

In the area of auxiliary medicine he has the special role of being a doctor or understanding medicine, nursing, pharmacology, drugs, elemental surgery, and emergency first aid.

The basic question in the technical preparation of the urban guerrilla is nevertheless to know how to handle arms such as the machine gun, revolver, automatic, FAL, various types of shotguns, carbines, mortars, bazookas, etc.

A knowledge of various types of ammunition and explosives is another aspect to consider. Among the explosives, dynamite must be well understood. The use of incendiary bombs, of smoke bombs, and other types are indispensable prior knowledge.

To know how to make and repair arms, prepare Molotov cocktails, grenades, mines, homemade destructive devices, how to blow up bridges, tear up and put out of service rails and sleepers, these are requisites in the technical preparation of the urban guerrilla that can never be considered unimportant.

The highest level of preparation for the urban guerrilla is the center for technical training. But only the guerrilla who has already passed the preliminary examination can go on to this school—that is to say, one who has passed the proof of fire in revolutionary action, in actual combat against the enemy.

The Urban Guerrilla's Arms

The urban guerrilla's arms are light arms, easily exchanged, usually captured from the enemy, purchased, or made on the spot.

Light arms have the advantage of fast handling and easy transport. In general, light arms are characterized as short barrelled. This includes many automatic arms.

Automatic and semiautomatic arms considerably increase the fighting power of the urban guerrilla. The disadvantage of this type of arm for us is the difficulty in controlling it, resulting in wasted rounds or in a prodigious use of ammunition, compensated for only by optimal aim and firing precision. Men who are poorly trained convert automatic weapons into an ammunition drain.

Experience has shown that the basic arm of the urban guerrilla is the light machine gun. This arm, in addition to being efficient and easy to shoot in an urban area, has the advantage of being greatly respected by the enemy. The guerrilla must know thoroughly how to handle the machine gun, now so popular and indispensable to the Brazilian urban guerrilla.

The ideal machine gun for the urban guerrilla is the Ina 45 calibre. Other types of machine guns of different calibres can be used—understanding, of course, the problem of ammunition. Thus it is preferable that the industrial potential of the urban guerrilla permit the production of a single machine gun so that the ammunition used can be standardized.

Each firing group of urban guerrillas must have a machine gun managed by a good marksman. The other components of the group must be armed with .38 revolvers, our standard arm. The .32 is also useful for those who want to participate. But the .38 is preferable since its impact usually puts the enemy out of action.

Hand grenades and conventional smoke bombs can be considered light arms, with defensive power for cover and withdrawal.

Long barrel arms are more difficult for the urban guerrilla to transport and attract much attention because of their size. Among the long barrel arms are the FAL, the Mauser guns or rifles, hunting guns such as the Winchester, and others.

Shotguns can be useful if used at close range and point blank. They are useful even for a poor shot, especially at night when precision isn't much help. A pressure airgun can be useful for training in marksmanship. Bazookas and mortars can also be used in action but the conditions for using them have to be prepared and the people who use them must be trained.

The urban guerrilla should not try to base his actions on the use of heavy arms, which have major drawbacks in a type of fighting that demands lightweight weapons to insure mobility and speed.

Homemade weapons are often as efficient as the best arms produced in conventional factories, and even a cut-off shotgun is a good arm for the urban guerrilla.

The urban guerrilla's role as gunsmith has a fundamental importance. As gunsmith he takes care of the arms, knows how to repair them, and in many cases can set up a small shop for improvising and producing efficient small arms.

Work in metallurgy and on the mechanical lathe are basic skills the urban guerrilla should incorporate into his industrial planning, which is the construction of homemade weapons.

This construction and courses in explosives and sabotage must be organized. The primary materials for practice in these courses must be obtained ahead of time to prevent an incomplete apprenticeship—that is to say, so as to leave no room for experimentation.

Molotov cocktails, gasoline, homemade contrivances such as catapults and mortars for firing explosives, grenades made of tubes and cans, smoke bombs, mines, conventional explosives such as dynamite and potassium chloride, plastic explosives, gelatine capsules, ammunition of every kind are indispensable to the success of the urban guerrilla's mission.

The method of obtaining the necessary materials and munitions will be to buy them or to take them by force in expropriation actions especially planned and carried out.

The urban guerrilla will be careful not to keep explosives and materials that can cause accidents around for very long, but will try always to use them immediately on their destined targets.

The urban guerrilla's arms and his ability to maintain them constitute his fire power. By taking advantage of modern arms and introducing innovations in his fire power and in the use of certain arms, the urban guerrilla can change many of the tactics of city warfare. An example of this was the innovation made by the urban guerrillas in Brazil when they introduced the machine gun in their attacks on banks.

When the massive use of uniform machine guns becomes possible, there will be new changes in urban guerrilla warfare tactics. The firing group that utilizes uniform weapons and corresponding ammunition, with reasonable support for their maintenance, will reach a considerable level of efficiency. The urban guerrilla increases his efficiency as he improves his firing potential.

The Shot: the Urban Guerrilla's Reason for Existence

The urban guerrilla's reason for existence, the basic condition in which he acts and survives, is to shoot. The urban guerrilla must know how to shoot well because it is required by his type of combat.

In conventional warfare, combat is generally at a distance with long range arms. In unconventional warfare, in which urban guerrilla warfare is included, the combat is at close range, often very close. To prevent his own extinction, the urban guerrilla has to shoot first and he cannot err in his shot. He cannot waste his ammunition because he doesn't have large amounts, so he must save it. Nor can he replace his ammunition quickly, since he is part of a small group in which each guerrilla has to take care of himself. The urban guerrilla can lose no time and must be able to shoot at once.

One fundamental fact which we want to emphasize fully and whose particular importance cannot be overestimated is that the urban guerrilla must not fire continuously, using up his ammunition. It may be that the enemy is not responding to the fire precisely because he is waiting until the guerrilla's ammunition is used up. At such a moment, without having time to replace his ammunition, the urban guerrilla faces a rain of enemy fire and can be taken prisoner or be killed.

In spite of the value of the surprise factor which many times makes it unnecessary for the urban guerrilla to use his arms, he cannot be allowed the luxury of entering combat without knowing how to shoot. And face to face with the enemy, he must always be moving from one position to another, because to stay in one position makes him a fixed target and, as such, very vulnerable.

The urban guerrilla's life depends on shooting, on his ability to handle his arms well and to avoid being hit. When we speak of shooting, we speak of marksmanship as well. Shooting must be learned until it becomes a reflex action on the part of the urban guerrilla.

To learn how to shoot and to have good aim, the urban guerrilla must train himself systematically, utilizing every apprenticeship method, shooting at targets, even in amusement parks and at home.

Shooting and marksmanship are the urban guerrilla's water and air. His perfection of the art of shooting makes him a special type of urban guerrilla—that is, a sniper, a category of solitary combatant indispensable in isolated actions. The sniper knows how to shoot, at close range and at long range, and his arms are appropriate for either type of shooting.

The Firing Group

In order to function, the urban guerrillas must be organized in small groups. A group of no more than four or five is called *the firing group*.

A minimum of two firing groups, separated and sealed off from other firing groups, directed and coordinated by one or two persons, this is what makes a *firing team*.

Within the firing group there must be complete confidence among the comrades. The best shot and the one who best knows how to manage the machine gun is the person in charge of operations.

The firing group plans and executes urban guerrilla actions, obtains and guards arms, studies and corrects its own tactics.

When there are tasks planned by the strategic command, these tasks take preference. But there is no such thing as a firing group without its own initiative. For this reason it is essential to avoid any rigidity in the organization in order to permit the greatest possible initiative on the part of the firing group. The old-type hierarchy, the style of the traditional left doesn't exist in our organization.

This means that, except for the priority of objectives set by the strategic command, any firing group can decide to assault a bank, to kidnap or to execute an agent of the dictatorship, a figure identified with the reaction, or a North American spy, and can carry out any kind of propaganda or war of nerves against the enemy without the need to consult the general command.

No firing group can remain inactive waiting for orders from above. Its obligation is to act. Any single urban guerrilla who wants to establish a firing group and begin action can do so and thus become a part of the organization.

This method of action eliminates the need for knowing who is carrying out which actions, since there is free initiative and the only important point is to increase substantially the volume of urban guerrilla activity in order to wear out the government and force it onto the defensive.

The firing group is the instrument of organized action. Within it, guerrilla operations and tactics are planned, launched, and carried through to success.

The general command counts on the firing groups to carry out objectives of a strategic nature, and to do so in any part of the country. For its part, it helps the firing groups with their difficulties and their needs.

The organization is an indestructible network of firing groups, and of coordinations among them, that functions simply and practically with a general command that also participates in the the attacks; an organization which exists for no purpose other than pure and simple revolutionary action.

The Logistics of the Urban Guerrilla

Conventional logistics can be expressed by the formula CCEM:

C —food *(comida)*
C —fuel *(combustivel)*
E —equipment
M—ammunition *(munições)*

Conventional logistics refer to the maintenance problems for an army or a regular armed force, transported in vehicles with fixed bases and supply lines.

Urban guerrillas, on the contrary, are not an army but small armed groups, intentionally fragmented. They have no vehicles nor fixed bases. Their supply lines are precarious and insufficient, and have no established base except in the rudimentary sense of an arms factory within a house.

While the goal of conventional logistics is to supply the war needs of the gorillas to be used to repress urban and rural rebellion, urban guerrilla logistics aim at sustaining operations and tactics which have nothing in common with a conventional war and are directed against the military dictatorship and North American domination of the country.

For the urban guerrilla, who starts from nothing and has no support at the beginning, logistics are expressed by the formula MDAME, which is:

M—mechanization
D—money *(dinheiro)*
A—arms
M—ammunition *(munições)*
E—explosives

Revolutionary logistics takes mechanization as one of its bases. Nevertheless, mechanization is inseparable from the driver. The urban guerrilla driver is as important as the urban guerrilla machine gunner. Without either, the machines do not work, and as such the automobile like the machine gun becomes a dead thing. An experienced driver is not made in one day and the apprenticeship must begin early. Every good urban guerrilla must be a good driver. As to the vehicle, the urban guerrilla must expropriate what he needs.

When he already has resources, the urban guerrilla can combine the expropriation of vehicles with other methods of acquisition.

Money, arms, ammunition and explosives, and automobiles as well, must be expropriated. And the urban guerrilla must rob banks and armories and seize explosives and ammunition wherever he finds them.

None of these operations is undertaken for just one purpose. Even when the assault is for money, the arms that the guards bear must also be taken.

Expropriation is the first step in the organization of our logistics, which itself assumes an armed and permanently mobile character.

The second step is to reinforce and extend logistics, resorting to ambushes and traps in which the enemy will be surprised and his arms, ammunition, vehicles, and other resources can be captured.

Once he has the arms, ammunition, and explosives, one of the most serious logistics problems the urban guerrilla faces at any time and in any situation is a hiding place in which to leave the material and appropriate means for transporting it and assembling it where it is needed. This has to be accomplished even when the enemy is on the lookout and has the roads blocked.

The knowledge that the urban guerrilla has of the terrain, and the devices he uses or is capable of using, such as guides especially prepared and recruited for this mission, are the basic elements in the solution of the eternal logistics problem the revolutionary faces.

The Technique of the Urban Guerrilla

In its most general sense, technique is the combination of methods man uses to carry out any activity. The activity of the urban guerrilla consists in waging guerrilla warfare and psychological warfare.

The urban guerrilla technique has five basic components:

a) one part is related to the specific characteristics of the situation;

b) one part is related to the requisites that match these characteristics, requisites represented by a series of initial advantages without which the urban guerrilla cannot achieve his objectives;

c) one part concerns certain and definite objectives in the actions initiated by the urban guerrilla;

d) one part is related to the types and characteristic modes of action for the urban guerrilla;

e) one part is concerned with the urban guerrilla's methods of carrying out his specific actions.

Characteristics of the Urban Guerrilla's Technique

The technique of the urban guerrilla has the following characteristics:

a) it is an aggressive technique, or in other words, it has an offensive character. As is well known, defensive action means death for us. Since we are inferior to the enemy in fire power and have neither his resources nor his power force, we cannot defend ourselves against an offensive or a concentrated attack by the gorillas. And that is the reason why our urban technique can never be permanent, can never defend a fixed base nor remain in any one spot waiting to repel the circle of reaction;

b) it is a technique of attack and retreat by which we preserve our forces;

c) it is a technique that aims at the development of urban guerrilla warfare, whose function will be to wear out, demoralize, and distract the enemy forces, permitting the emergence and survival of rural guerrilla warfare which is destined to play the decisive role in the revolutionary war.

The Initial Advantages of the Urban Guerrilla

The dynamics of urban guerrilla warfare lie in the urban guerrilla's violent clash with the military and police forces of the dictatorship. In this clash, the police have the superiority. The urban guerrilla has inferior forces. The paradox is that the urban guerrilla, although weaker, is nevertheless the attacker.

The military and police forces, for their part, respond to the attack, by mobilizing and concentrating infinitely superior forces in the persecution and destruction of the urban guerrilla. He can only avoid defeat if he counts on the initial advantages he has and knows how to exploit

them to the end to compensate for his weaknesses and lack of matériel.
The initial advantages are:

1) he must take the enemy by surprise;

2) he must know the terrain of the encounter better than the enemy;

3) he must have greater mobility and speed than the police and the
other repressive forces;

4) his information service must be better than the enemy's;

5) he must be in command of the situation and demonstrate a decisiveness so great that everyone on our side is inspired and never thinks
of hesitating, while on the other side the enemy is stunned and incapable of responding.

Surprise

To compensate for the general weakness and shortage of arms compared to the enemy, the urban guerrilla uses surprise. The enemy has no
way to fight surprise and becomes confused or is destroyed.

When urban guerrilla warfare broke out in Brazil, experience proved
that surprise was essential to the success of any urban guerrilla operation.

The technique of surprise is based on four essential requisites:

a) we know the situation of the enemy we are going to attack, usually by means of precise information and meticulous observation,
while the enemy does not know he is going to be attacked and knows
nothing about the attacker;

b) we know the force of the enemy that is going to be attacked and
the enemy knows nothing about our force;

c) attacking by surprise, we save and conserve our forces, while the
enemy is unable to do the same and is left at the mercy of events;

d) we determine the hour and the place of the attack, fix its duration,
and establish its objective. The enemy remains ignorant of all this.

Knowledge of the Terrain

The urban guerrilla's best ally is the terrain and because this is so he
must know it like the palm of his hand.

To have the terrain as an ally means to know how to use with intelligence its unevenness, its high and its low points, its turns, its irregularities, its regular and its secret passages, abandoned areas, its thickets, etc.,

taking maximum advantage of all this for the success of armed actions, escapes, retreats, cover, and hiding places.

Its impasses and narrow spots, its gorges, its streets under repair, police control points, military zones and closed off streets, the entrances and exits of tunnels and those that the enemy can close off, viaducts to be crossed, corners controlled by the police or watched, its lights and signals, all this must be thoroughly known and studied in order to avoid fatal errors.

Our problem is to get through and to know where and how to hide, leaving the enemy bewildered in areas he doesn't know.

Familiar with the avenues, streets, alleys, ins and outs, and corners of the urban centers, its paths and shortcuts, its empty lots, its underground passages, its pipes and sewer system, the urban guerrilla safely crosses through the irregular and difficult terrain unfamiliar to the police, where they can be surprised in a fatal ambush or trapped at any moment.

Because he knows the terrain the guerrilla can go through it on foot, on bicycle, in automobile, jeep, or truck and never be trapped. Acting in small groups with only a few people, the guerrillas can reunite at an hour and place determined beforehand, following up the attack with new guerrilla operations, or evading the police circle and disorienting the enemy with their unprecedented audacity.

It is an insoluble problem for the police in the labyrinthian terrain of the urban guerrilla, to get someone they can't see, to repress someone they can't catch, to close in on someone they can't find.

Our experience is that the ideal urban guerrilla is one who operates in his own city and knows thoroughly its streets, its neighborhoods, its transit problems, and other peculiarities.

The guerrilla outsider, who comes to a city whose corners are unfamiliar to him, is a weak spot and if he is assigned certain operations, can endanger them. To avoid grave errors, it is necessary for him to get to know well the layout of the streets.

Mobility and Speed

To insure a mobility and speed that the police cannot match, the urban guerrilla needs the following prerequisites:

a) mechanization;
b) knowledge of the terrain;
c) a rupture or suspension of enemy communications and transport;
d) light arms.

By carefully carrying through operations that last only a few moments, and leaving the site in mechanized vehicles, the urban guerrilla beats a rapid retreat, escaping pursuit.

The urban guerrilla must know the way in detail and, in this sense, must go through the schedule ahead of time as a training to avoid entering alleyways that have no exit, or running into traffic jams, or becoming paralyzed by the Transit Department's traffic signals.

The police pursue the urban guerrilla blindly without knowing which road he is using for his escape.

While the urban guerrilla quickly flees because he knows the terrain, the police lose the trail and give up the chase.

The urban guerrilla must launch his operations far from the logistics base of the police. An initial advantage of this method of operation is that it places us at a reasonable distance from the possibility of pursuit, which facilitates the evasion.

In addition to this necessary precaution, the urban guerrilla must be concerned with the enemy's communication system. The telephone is the primary target in preventing the enemy from having access to information by knocking out his communication system.

Even if he knows about the guerrilla operation, the enemy depends on modern transport for his logistics support, and his vehicles necessarily lose time carrying him through the heavy traffic of the large cities.

It is clear that the tangled and treacherous traffic is a disadvantage for the enemy, as it would be for us if we were not ahead of him.

If we want to have a safe margin of security and be certain to leave no tracks for the future, we can adopt the following methods:

a) purposely intercept the police with other vehicles or by apparently casual inconveniences and damages; but in this case the vehicles in question should not be legal nor should they have real license numbers;

b) obstruct the road with fallen trees, rocks, ditches, false traffic signs, dead ends or detours, and other ingenious methods:

c) place homemade mines in the way of the police, use gasoline, or throw Molotov cocktails to set their vehicles on fire;

d) set off a burst of machine gun fire or arms such as the FAL aimed at the motor and the tires of the cars engaged in pursuit.

With the arrogance typical of the police and the military fascist authorities, the enemy will come to fight us with heavy guns and equipment and with elaborate maneuvers by men armed to the teeth. The urban guerrilla must respond to this with light weapons easily transported, so he can always escape with maximum speed, without ever accepting open fighting. The urban guerrilla has no mission other than to attack and retreat.

We would leave ourselves open to the most stunning defeats if we burdened ourselves with heavy arms and with the tremendous weight of the ammunition necessary to fire them, at the same time losing our precious gift of mobility.

When the enemy fights against us with cavalry we are at no disadvantage as long as we are mechanized. The automobile goes faster than the horse. From within the car we also have the target of the mounted police, knocking them down with machine gun and revolver fire or with Molotov cocktails and grenades.

On the other hand, it is not so difficult for an urban guerrilla on foot to make a target of a policeman on horseback. Moreover, ropes across the streets, marbles, cork stoppers are very efficient methods of making them both fall. The great advantage of the mounted police is that he presents the urban guerrilla with two excellent targets: the horse and its rider.

Apart from being faster than the horseman, the helicopter has no better chance in pursuit. If the horse is too slow compared to the urban guerrilla's automobile, the helicopter is too fast. Moving at 200 kilometers an hour it will never succeed in hitting from above a target lost among the crowds and the street vehicles, nor can it land in public streets in order to catch someone. At the same time, whenever it tries to fly low, it will be excessively vulnerable to the fire of the urban guerrilla.

Information

The possibilities that the government has for discovering and destroying the urban guerrillas lessen as the potential of the dictatorship's enemies becomes greater and more concentrated among the popular masses.

This concentration of opponents of the dictatorship plays a very important role in providing information as to moves on the part of the police and men in government, as well as in hiding our activities. The enemy can also be thrown off by false information, which is worse for him because it is a tremendous waste.

By whatever means, the sources of information at the disposal of the urban guerrilla are potentially better than those of the police. The enemy is observed by the people, but he does not know who among the people transmits information to the urban guerrilla. The military and the police are hated for the injustices they commit against the people, and this facilitates obtaining information prejudical to the activities of government agents.

The information, which is only a small area of popular support, represents an extraordinary potential in the hands of the urban guerrilla. The creation of an intelligence service with an organized structure is a basic need for us. The urban guerrilla has to have essential information about the plans and movements of the enemy, where they are, and how they move, the resources of the banking network, the means of communication, and the secret moves the enemy makes.

The trustworthy information passed along to the urban guerrilla represents a well-aimed blow at the dictatorship. It has no way to defend itself in the face of an important leak that jeopardizes its interests and facilitates our destructive attack.

The enemy also wants to know what steps we are taking so he can destroy us or prevent us from acting. In this sense the danger of betrayal is present and the enemy encourages betrayal or infiltrates spies into the organization. The urban guerrilla's technique against this enemy tactic is to denounce publicly the traitors, spies, informers, and provocateurs.

Since our struggle takes place among the masses and depends on their sympathy—while the government has a bad reputation because of its brutality, corruption, and incompetence—the informers, spies, traitors, and the police come to be enemies of the people without supporters, denounced to the urban guerrillas, and, in many cases, properly punished.

For his part the urban guerrilla must not evade the duty—once he knows who the spy or informer is—of wiping him out physically. This is the correct method, approved by the people, and it minimizes considerably the incidence of infiltration or enemy spying.

For the complete success of the battle against spies and informers, it is essential to organize a counterespionage or counterintelligence service. Nevertheless, as far as information is concerned, it cannot all be reduced to a question of knowing the enemy's moves and avoiding the infiltration of spies. Information must be broad, it must embrace everything, including the most insignificant matters. There is a technique of obtaining information, and the urban guerrilla must master it. Following this technique, information is obtained naturally, as a part of the life of the people.

The urban guerrilla, living in the midst of the people and moving about among them, must be attentive to all types of conversations and human relations, learning how to disguise his interest with great skill and judgment.

In places where people work, study, live, it is easy to collect all kinds of information on payments, business, plans of all types, points of view, opinions, people's state of mind, trips, interiors of buildings, offices and rooms, operation centers, etc.

Observation, investigation, reconnaissance, and exploration of the terrain are also excellent sources of information. The urban guerrilla never goes anywhere absentmindedly and without revolutionary precaution, always on the lookout lest something occur. Eyes and ears open, senses alert, his memory engraved with everything necessary, now or in the future, to the uninterrupted activity of the fighter

Careful reading of the press with particular attention to the organs of mass communication, the investigation of accumulated data, the transmission of news and everything of note, a persistence in being informed and in informing others, all this makes up the intricate and immensely complicated question of information which gives the urban guerrilla a decisive advantage.

Decision

It is not enough for the urban guerrilla to have in his favor surprise, speed, knowledge of the terrain, and information. He must also demonstrate his command of any situation and a capacity for decision without which all other advantages will prove useless.

It is impossible to carry out any action, however well planned, if the urban guerrilla turns out to be indecisive, uncertain, irresolute.

Even an action successfully begun can end in defeat if the command of the situation and the capacity for decision falter in the middle of the actual execution of the plan. When this command of the situation and a capacity for decision are absent, the void is filled with vacillation and terror. The enemy takes advantage of this failure and is able to liquidate us.

The secret for the success of any operation, simple or complicated, easy or difficult, is to rely on determined men. Strictly speaking, there are no easy operations. All must be carried out with the same care exercised in the case of the most difficult, beginning with the choice of the human element, which means relying on leadership and capacity for decision in every test.

One can see ahead of time whether an action will be successful or not by the way its participants act during the preparatory period. Those who are behind, who fail to make designated contacts, are easily confused, forget things, fail to complete the basic elements of the work, possibly are indecisive men and can be a danger. It is better not to include them.

Decision means to put into practice the plan that has been devised with determination, with audacity, and with an absolute firmness. It takes only one person who vacillates to lose all.

Objectives of the Urban Guerrilla's Actions

With his technique developed and established, the urban guerrilla bases himself on models of action leading to attack and, in Brazil, with the following objectives:

a) to threaten the triangle in which the Brazilian state system and North American domination are maintained in Brazil, a triangle whose points are Rio, São Paulo, and Belo Horizonte and whose base is the axle Rio-São Paulo, where the giant industrial-financial-economic-political-cultural-military-police complex that holds the entire decisive power of the country is located;

b) to weaken the local guards or the security system of the dictatorship, given the fact that we are attacking and the gorillas defending, which means catching the government in a defensive position with its troops immobilized in defense of the entire complex of national maintenance, with its ever-present fears of an attack on its strategic nerve centers, and without ever knowing where, how, and when that attack will come;

c) to attack on every side with many different armed groups, few in number, each self-contained and operating separately, to disperse the government forces in their pursuit of a thoroughly fragmented organization instead of offering the dictatorship the opportunity to concentrate its forces of repression on the destruction of one tightly organized system operating throughout the country;

d) to give proof of its combativeness, decision, firmness, determination, and persistence in the attack on the military dictatorship in order to permit all malcontents to follow our example and fight with urban guerrilla tactics. Meanwhile, the government, with all its problems, incapable of halting guerrilla operations in the city, will lose time and suffer endless attrition and will finally be forced to pull back its repressive troops in order to mount guard over the banks, industries, armories, military barracks, prisons, public offices, radio and television stations, North American firms, gas storage tanks, oil refineries, ships, airplanes, ports, airports, hospitals, health centers, blood banks, stores, garages, embassies, residences of outstanding members of the regime, such as ministers and generals, police stations, and official organizations, etc.;

e) to increase urban guerrilla disturbances gradually in an endless ascendancy of unforeseen actions such that the government troops cannot leave the urban area to pursue the guerrillas in the interior without running the risk of abandoning the cities and permitting rebellion to increase on the coast as well as in the interior of the country;

f) to oblige the army and the police, with the commanders and their assistants, to change the relative comfort and tranquillity of their barracks and their usual rest, for a state of alarm and growing tension in the expectation of attack or in search of tracks that vanish without a trace;

g) to avoid open battle and decisive combat with the government, limiting the struggle to brief and rapid attacks with lightning results;

h) to assure for the urban guerrilla a maximum freedom of maneuvers and of action without ever relinquishing the use of armed violence, remaining firmly oriented toward helping the beginning of rural guerrilla warfare and supporting the construction of the revolutionary army for national liberation.

On the Types and Nature of Action Models for the Urban Guerrilla

In order to achieve the objectives previously enumerated, the urban guerrilla is obliged, in his technique, to follow an action whose nature is as different and as diversified as possible. The urban guerrilla does not arbitrarily choose this or that action model. Some actions are simple, others are complicated. The urban guerrilla without experience must be incorporated gradually into actions and operations that run from the simple to the complex. He begins with small missions and tasks until he becomes a completely experienced urban guerrilla.

Before any action, the urban guerrilla must think of the methods and the personnel at his disposal to carry out the action. Operations and actions that demand the urban guerrilla's technical preparation cannot be carried out by someone who lacks that technical skill. With these cautions, the action models which the urban guerrilla can carry out are the following:

a) assaults;

b) raids and penetrations;

c) occupations;
d) ambush;
e) street tactics;
f) strikes and work interruptions;
g) desertions, diversions, seizures, expropriations of arms, ammunition, explosives;
h) liberation of prisoners;
i) executions;
j) kidnappings;
k) sabotage;
l) terrorism;
m) armed propaganda;
n) war of nerves.

Assaults

Assault is the armed attack which we make to expropriate funds, liberate prisoners, capture explosives, machine guns, and other types of arms and ammunition.

Assaults can take place in broad daylight or at night.

Daytime assaults are made when the objective cannot be achieved at any other hour, as for example, the transport of money by the banks, which is not done at night.

Night assault is usually the most advantageous to the urban guerrilla. The ideal is for all assaults to take place at night when conditions for a surprise attack are most favorable and the darkness facilitates flight and hides the identity of the participants. The urban guerrilla must prepare himself, nevertheless, to act under all conditions, daytime as well as nighttime.

The most vulnerable targets for assault are the following:
a) credit establishments;
b) commercial and industrial enterprises, including the production of arms and explosives;
c) military establishments;
d) commissaries and police stations;
e) jails;
f) government property;
g) mass communication media;
h) North American firms and properties;
i) government vehicles, including military and police vehicles, trucks, armored vehicles, money carriers, trains, ships, and planes.

The assaults on establishments are of the same nature because in every case the property and buildings represent a fixed target.

Assaults on buildings are conceived as guerrilla operations, varied according to whether they are against banks, a commercial enterprise, industries, military camps, commissaries, prisons, radio stations, warehouses for imperialist firms, etc.

The assaults on vehicles—money-carriers, armored cars, trains, ships, airplanes—are of another nature since they are moving targets. The nature of the operations varies according to the situation and the possibility—that is, whether the target is stationary or moving.

Armored cars, including military cars, are not immune to mines. Obstructed roads, traps, ruses, interception of other vehicles, Molotov cocktails, shooting with heavy arms, are efficient methods of assaulting vehicles.

Heavy vehicles, grounded planes, anchored ships can be seized and their crews and guards overcome. Airplanes in flight can be diverted from their course by guerrilla action or by one person.

Ships and trains in movement can be assaulted or taken by guerrilla operations in order to capture the arms and munitions or to prevent troop deployment.

The Bank Assault as Popular Model

The most popular assault model is the bank assault. In Brazil, the urban guerrilla has begun a type of organized assault on the banks as a guerrilla operation. Today this type of assault is widely used and has served as a sort of preliminary examination for the urban guerrilla in his apprenticeship for the techniques of revolutionary warfare.

Important innovations in the technique of assaulting banks have developed, guaranteeing flight, the withdrawal of money, and the anonymity of those involved. Among these innovations we cite shooting the tires of cars to prevent pursuit; locking people in the bank bathroom, making them sit on the floor; immobilizing the bank guards and removing their arms, forcing someone to open the coffer or the strong box; using disguises.

Attempts to install bank alarms, to use guards or electronic detection devices of U.S. origin, prove fruitless when the assault is political and is carried out according to urban guerrilla warfare technique. This technique tries to utilize new resources to meet the enemy's tactical changes, has access to a fire power that is growing every day, becomes increasingly astute and audacious, and uses a larger number of revolutionaries every time; all to guarantee the success of operations planned down to the last detail.

The bank assault is a typical expropriation. But, as is true in any kind of armed expropriatory action, the revolutionary is handicapped by a two-fold competition:

a) competition from the outlaw;

b) competition from the right-wing counterrevolutionary.

This competition produces confusion, which is reflected in the people's uncertainty. It is up to the urban guerrilla to prevent this from happening, and to accomplish this he must use two methods:

a) he must avoid the outlaw's technique, which is one of unnecessary violence and appropriation of goods and possessions belonging to the people;

b) he must use the assault for propaganda purposes, at the very moment it is taking place, and later distribute material, leaflets, every possible means of explaining the objectives and the principles of the urban guerrilla as expropriator of the government, the ruling classes, and imperialism.

Raids and Penetration

Raids and penetrations are quick attacks on establishments located in neighborhoods or even in the center of the city, such as small military units, commissaries, hospitals, to cause trouble, seize arms, punish and terrorize the enemy, take reprisal, or rescue wounded prisoners, or those hospitalized under police vigilance.

Raids and penetrations are also made on garages and depots to destroy vehicles and damage installations, especially if they are North American firms and property.

When they take place on certain stretches of the highway or in certain distant neighborhoods, the raids can serve to force the enemy to move great numbers of troops, a totally useless effort since he will find nobody there to fight.

When they are carried out in certain houses, offices, archives, or public offices, their purpose is to capture or search for secret papers and documents with which to denounce involvements, compromises, and the corruption of men in government, their dirty deals and criminal transactions with the North Americans.

Raids and penetrations are most effective if they are carried out at night.

Occupations

Occupations are a type of attack carried out when the urban guerrilla stations himself in specific establishments and locations for a temporary resistance against the enemy or for some propaganda purpose.

The occupation of factories and schools during strikes or at other times is a method of protest or of distracting the enemy's attention.

The occupation of radio stations is for propaganda purposes.

Occupation is a highly effective model for action but, in order to prevent losses and material damage to our ranks, it is always a good idea to count on the possibility of withdrawal. It must always be meticulously planned and carried out at the opportune moment.

Occupation always has a time limit and the faster it is completed the better.

Ambush

Ambushes are attacks typified by surprise when the enemy is trapped across a road or when he makes a police net surrounding a house or an estate. A false message can bring the enemy to the spot where he falls into the trap.

The principal object of the ambush tactic is to capture enemy arms and punish him with death.

Ambushes to halt passenger trains are for propaganda purposes and, when they are troop trains, the object is to annihilate the enemy and seize his arms.

The urban guerrilla sniper is the kind of fighter especially suited for ambush because he can hide easily in the irregularities of the terrain, on the roofs and tops of buildings and apartments under construction. From windows and dark places, he can take careful aim at his chosen target.

Ambush has devastating effects on the enemy, leaving him unnerved, insecure, and fearful.

Street Tactics

Street tactics are used to fight the enemy in the streets, utilizing the participation of the masses against him.

In 1968 the Brazilian students used excellent street tactics against police troops, such as marching down streets against traffic, utilizing slings and marbles as arms against the mounted police.

Other street tactics consist in constructing barricades; pulling up paving blocks and hurling them at the police; throwing bottles, bricks, paperweights, and other projectiles from the tops of apartment and office buildings against the police; using buildings under construction for flight, for hiding, and for supporting surprise attacks.

It is equally necessary to know how to respond to enemy tactics. When the police troops come protected with helmets to defend themselves against flying objects, we have to divide ourselves into two teams: one to attack the enemy from the front, the other to attack him in the rear, withdrawing one as the other goes into action to prevent the first from becoming a target for projectiles hurled by the second.

By the same token it is important to know how to respond to the police net. When the police designate certain of their men to go into the masses to arrest a demonstrator, a larger group of urban guerrillas must surround the police group, disarming and beating them and at the same time letting the prisoner escape. This urban guerrilla operation is called the *net within the net*.

When the police net is formed at a school building, a factory, a place where the masses assemble, or some other point, the urban guerrilla must not give up or allow himself to be taken by surprise. To make his net work the enemy is obliged to transport the police in vehicles and special cars to occupy strategic points in the streets in order to invade the building or chosen locale. The urban guerrilla, for his part, must never clear a building or an area and meet in it without first knowing its exits, the way to break the circle, the strategic points that the police might occupy, and the roads that inevitably lead into the net, and he must hold other strategic points from which to strike at the enemy.

The roads followed by the police vehicles must be mined at key points along the way and at forced stopping points. When the mines explode, the vehicles will fly into the air. The police will be caught in the trap and will suffer losses or will be victims of ambush. The net must be broken by escape routes unknown to the police. The rigorous planning of the retreat is the best way of frustrating any encircling effort on the part of the enemy.

When there is no possibility of a flight plan, the urban guerrilla must not hold meetings, assemblies, or do anything else since to do so will prevent him from breaking through the net the enemy will surely try to throw around him.

Street tactics have revealed a new type of urban guerrilla, the urban guerrilla who participates in mass demonstrations. This is the type we designate as the urban guerrilla demonstrator, who joins the ranks and participates in popular marches with specific and definite aims.

These aims consist in hurling stones and projectiles of every type, using gasoline to start fires, using the police as a target for their fire arms, capturing police arms, kidnapping agents of the enemy and provocateurs, shooting with careful aim at the henchmen torturers and the police chiefs who come in special cars with false plates in order not to attract attention.

The urban guerrilla demonstrator shows groups in the mass demonstration the flight route if that is necessary. He plants mines, throws Molotov cocktails, prepares ambushes and explosions.

The urban guerrilla demonstrator must also initiate the *net within the net*, going through government vehicles, official cars, and police vehicles before turning them over or setting them on fire, to see if any of them have money and arms.

Snipers are very good for mass demonstrations and, along with the urban guerrilla demonstrators, can play a valuable role.

Hidden at strategic points, the snipers have complete success, using shotguns, machine guns, etc. whose fire and ricocheting easily cause losses among the enemy.

Strikes and Work Interruptions

The strike is a model of action employed by the urban guerrilla in work centers and schools to damage the enemy by stopping work and study activities. Because it is one of the weapons most feared by the exploiters and oppressors, the enemy uses tremendous fighting power and incredible violence against it. The strikers are taken to prison, suffer beatings, and many of them wind up assassinated.

The urban guerrilla must prepare the strike in such a way as to leave no tracks or clues that identify the leaders of the action. A strike is successful when it is organized through the action of a small group, if it is carefully prepared in secret and by the most clandestine methods.

Arms, ammunition, Molotovs, homemade weapons of destruction and attack, all this must be supplied beforehand in order to meet the enemy. So that it can do the greatest possible damage, it is a good idea to study and put into effect a sabotage plan.

Work and study interruptions, although they are of brief duration, cause severe damage to the enemy. It is enough for them to crop up at different points and in different sections of the same area, disrupting daily life, occurring endlessly one after the other, in authentic guerrilla fashion.

In strikes or simple work interruptions, the urban guerrilla has recourse to occupation or penetration of the locale or can simply make a raid. In that case his objective is to take hostages, to capture prisoners, or to kidnap enemy agents and propose an exchange for the arrested strikers.

In certain cases, strikes and brief work interruptions can offer an excellent opportunity for preparing ambushes or traps whose aim is the physical liquidation of the cruel, bloody police.

The basic fact is that the enemy suffers losses and material and moral damage, and is weakened by the action.

Desertions, Diversions, Seizures, Expropriations of Arms, Ammunition, Explosives

Desertion and the diversion of arms are actions effected in military camps, ships, military hospitals, etc. The urban guerrilla soldier, chief, sergeant, subofficial, and official must desert at the most opportune moment with modern arms and ammunition to hand them over for the use of the Brazilian revolution.

One of the opportune moments is when the military urban guerrilla is called upon to pursue and to fight his guerrilla comrades outside the military quarters. Instead of following the orders of the gorillas, the military urban guerrilla must join the revolutionaries by handing over the arms and ammunition he carries, or the military plane he pilots.

The advantage of this method is that the revolutionaries receive arms and ammunition from the army, the navy, and the air force, the military police, the civilian guard, or the firemen without any great work, since it reaches their hands by government transport.

Other opportunities may occur in the barracks, and the military urban guerrilla must always be alert to this. In case of carelessness on the part of the commanders or in other favorable conditions, such as bureaucratic attitudes and behavior or relaxation of discipline on the part of sublieutenants and other internal personnel, the military urban guerrilla must no longer wait but must try to advise the organizations and desert alone or accompanied, but with as large a supply of arms as possible.

With information from and participation of the military urban guerrilla, raids on barracks and other military establishments for the purpose of capturing arms can be organized.

When there is no possibility of deserting and taking arms and ammunition, the military urban guerrilla must engage in sabotage, starting explosions and fires in munitions and gunpowder.

This technique of deserting with arms and ammunition, of raiding and sabotaging the military centers, is the best way of wearing out and demoralizing the gorillas and of leaving them confused.

The urban guerrilla's purpose in disarming an individual enemy is to capture his arms. These arms are usually in the hands of sentinels or others whose task is guard duty or repression.

The capture of arms may be accompanied by violent means or by astuteness and by tricks or traps. When the enemy is disarmed, he must be searched for arms other than those already taken from him. If we are careless, he can use the arms that were not seized to shoot the urban guerrilla.

The seizure of arms is an efficient method of acquiring machine guns, the urban guerrilla's most important arms.

When we carry out small operations or actions to seize arms and ammunition, the material captured may be for personal use or for armaments and supplies for the firing groups.

The necessity to provide firing power for the urban guerrilla is so great that in order to take off from zero point we often have to purchase one weapon, divert or capture a single arm. The basic point is to begin, and to begin with a great spirit of decisiveness and of boldness. The possession of a single arm multiplies our forces.

In a bank assault, we must be careful to seize the arm or arms of the bank guard. The remainder of the arms we find with the treasurer, the bank teller, or the manager must also be seized ahead of time.

The other method we can use to capture arms is the preparation of ambushes against the police and the cars they use to move around in.

Quite often we succeed in capturing arms in the police commissaries as a result of raids from outside.

The expropriation of arms, ammunition, and explosives is the urban guerrilla's goal in assaulting commercial houses, industries, and quarries.

Liberation of Prisoners

The liberation of prisoners is an armed operation designed to free the jailed urban guerrilla. In daily struggle against the enemy, the urban guerrilla is subject to arrest and can be sentenced to unlimited years in jail. This does not mean that the revolutionary battle stops here. For the guerrilla, his experience is deepened by prison and continues even in the dungeons where he is held.

The imprisoned urban guerrilla views jail as a terrain he must dominate and understand in order to free himself by a guerrilla operation.

There is no prison, either on an island, in a city penitentiary, or on a farm, that is impregnable to the slyness, the cleverness, and the firing potential of the revolutionaries.

The urban guerrilla who is free views the penal establishments of the enemy as the inevitable site of guerrilla action designed to liberate his ideological brothers from prison.

It is this combination of *the urban guerrilla in freedom and the urban guerrilla in jail* that results in the armed operations we refer to as the liberation of prisoners.

The guerrilla operations that can be used in liberating prisoners are the following:

a) riots in penal establishments, in correctional colonies and islands, or on transport or prison ships;

b) assaults on urban or rural penitentiaries, houses of detention, commissaries, prisoner depots, or any other permanent, occasional, or temporary place where prisoners are held;

c) assaults on prisoner transport trains and cars;

d) raids and penetrations of prisons;

e) ambushing of guards who are moving prisoners.

Execution

Execution is the killing of a North American spy, of an agent of the dictatorship, of a police torturer, of a fascist personality in the government involved in crimes and persecutions against patriots, of a stool pigeon, informer, police agent, or police provocateur.

Those who go to the police of their own free will to make denunciations and accusations, who supply clues and information and finger people, must also be executed when they are caught by the urban guerrilla.

Execution is a secret action in which the least possible number of urban guerrillas are involved. In many cases, the execution can be carried out by one sniper, patiently, alone and unknown, and operating in absolute secrecy and in cold blood.

Kidnapping

Kidnapping is capturing and holding in a secret spot a police agent, a North American spy, a political personality, or a notorious and dangerous enemy of the revolutionary movement.

Kidnapping is used to exchange or liberate imprisoned revolutionary comrades, or to force suspension of torture in the jail cells of the military dictatorship.

The kidnapping of personalities who are known artists, sports figures, or are outstanding in some other field, but who have evidenced no political interest, can be a useful form of propaganda for the revolutionary and patriotic principles of the urban guerrilla provided it occurs under special circumstances, and the kidnapping is handled so that the public sympathizes with it and accepts it.

The kidnapping of North American residents or visitors in Brazil constitutes a form of protest against the penetration and domination of United States imperialism in our country.

Sabotage

Sabotage is a highly destructive type of attack using very few persons and sometimes requiring only one to accomplish the desired result. When the urban guerrilla uses sabotage the first phase is isolated sabotage. Then comes the phase of dispersed and generalized sabotage, carried out by the people.

Well-executed sabotage demands study, planning, and careful execution. A characteristic form of sabotage is explosion using dynamite, fire, and the placing of mines.

A little sand, a trickle of any kind of combustible, a poor lubrication, a screw removed, a short circuit, pieces of wood or of iron, can cause irreparable damage.

The objective of sabotage is to hurt, to damage, to make useless, and to destroy vital enemy points such as the following:

a) the economy of the country;
b) agricultural or industrial production;
c) transport and communication systems;
d) the military and police systems and their establishments and deposits;
e) the repressive military-police system;
f) the firms and properties of North Americans in the country.

The urban guerrilla should endanger the economy of the country, particularly its economic and financial aspects, such as its domestic and foreign commercial network, its exchange and banking systems, its tax collection systems, and others.

Public offices, centers of government services, government warehouses, are easy targets for sabotage.

Nor will it be easy to prevent the sabotage of agricultural and industrial production by the urban guerrilla, with his thorough knowledge of the local situation.

Industrial workers acting as urban guerrillas are excellent industrial saboteurs since they, better than anyone, understand the industry, the factory, the machine, or the part most likely to destroy an entire operation, doing far more damage than a poorly informed layman could do.

With respect to the enemy's transport and communications systems, beginning with railway traffic, it is necessary to attack them systematically with sabotage arms.

The only caution is against causing death and fatal injury to passengers, especially regular commuters on suburban and long-distance trains.

Attacks on freight trains, rolling or stationary stock, stoppage of military transport and communication systems, these are the major sabotage objectives in this area.

Sleepers can be damaged and pulled up, as can rails. A tunnel blocked by a barrier after an explosion, an obstruction by a derailed car, cause tremendous harm.

The derailment of a cargo train carrying fuel is of major damage to the enemy. So is dynamiting railway bridges. In a system where the weight and the size of the rolling equipment is enormous, it takes months for workers to repair or rebuild the destruction and damage.

As for highways, they can be obstructed by trees, stationary vehicles, ditches, dislocation of barriers by dynamite, and bridges blown up by explosion.

Ships can be damaged at anchor in seaports and river ports or in the shipyards. Airplanes can be destroyed or sabotaged on the ground.

Telephonic and telegraphic lines can be systematically damaged, their towers blown up, and their lines made useless.

Transport and communications must be sabotaged at once because the revolutionary war has already begun in Brazil and it is essential to impede the enemy's movement of troops and munitions.

Oil lines, fuel plants, depots for bombs and ammunition, powder magazines and arsenals, military camps, commissaries must become targets par excellence in sabotage operations, while vehicles, army trucks, and other military and police cars must be destroyed wherever they are found.

The military and police repression centers and their specific and specialized organs, must also claim the attention of the urban guerrilla saboteur.

North American firms and properties in the country, for their part, must become such frequent targets of sabotage that the volume of actions directed against them surpasses the total of all other actions against vital enemy points.

Terrorism

Terrorism is an action, usually involving the placement of a bomb or fire explosion of great destructive power, which is capable of effecting irreparable loss against the enemy.

Terrorism requires that the urban guerrilla should have an adequate theoretical and practical knowledge of how to make explosives.

The terroristic act, apart from the apparent facility with which it can be carried out, is no different from other urban guerrilla acts and actions whose success depends on the planning and determination of the revolutionary organization. It is an action the urban guerrilla must execute with the greatest cold bloodedness, calmness, and decision.

Although terrorism generally involves an explosion, there are cases in which it may also be carried out by execution and the systematic burning of installations, properties, and North American depots, plantations, etc. It is essential to point out the importance of fires and the construction of incendiary bombs such as gasoline bombs in the technique of revolutionary terrorism. Another thing is the importance of the material the urban guerrilla can persuade the people to expropriate in moments of hunger and scarcity resulting from the greed of the big commercial interests.

Terrorism is an arm the revolutionary can never relinquish.

Armed Propaganda

The coordination of urban guerrilla actions, including each armed action, is the principal way of making armed propaganda.

These actions, carried out with specific and determined objectives, inevitably become propaganda material for the mass communications system.

Bank assaults, ambushes, desertions and diverting of arms, the rescue of prisoners, executions, kidnappings, sabotage, terrorism, and the war of nerves, are all cases in point.

Airplanes diverted in flight by revolutionary action, moving ships and trains assaulted and seized by guerrillas, can also be solely for propaganda effects.

But the urban guerrilla must never fail to install a clandestine press and must be able to turn out mimeographed copies using alcohol or electric plates and other duplicating apparatus, expropriating what he cannot buy in order to produce small clandestine newspapers, pamphlets, flyers, and stamps for propaganda and agitation against the dictatorship.

The urban guerrilla engaged in clandestine printing facilitates enormously the incorporation of large numbers of people into the revolutionary struggle, by opening a permanent work front for those willing to carry on revolutionary propaganda, even when to do so means acting alone and risking their lives as revolutionaries.

With the existence of clandestine propaganda and agitational material, the inventive spirit of the urban guerrilla expands and creates catapults, artifacts, mortars, and other instruments with which to distribute the antigovernment pamphlets at a distance.

Tape recordings, the occupation of radio stations, and the use of loudspeakers, drawings on walls and in other inaccessible places are other forms of propaganda.

In using them, the urban guerrilla should give them the character of armed operations.

A consistent propaganda by letters sent to specific addresses, explaining the meaning of the urban guerrillas' armed actions, produces considerable results and is one method of influencing certain segments of the population.

Even this influence exercised in the heart of the people by every possible propaganda device revolving around the activity of the urban guerrilla does not indicate that our forces have everyone's support.

It it enough to win the support of a part of the people and this can be done by popularizing the following slogan: "Let he who does not wish to do anything for the revolutionaries, do nothing against them."

The War of Nerves

The war of nerves or psychological war is an aggressive technique, based on the direct or indirect use of mass means of communication and news transmitted orally in order to demoralize the government.

In psychological warfare, the government is always at a disadvantage since it imposes censorship on the mass media and winds up in a defensive position by not allowing anything against it to filter through.

At this point it becomes desperate, is involved in greater contradictions and loss of prestige, and loses time and energy in an exhausting effort at control which is subject to being broken at any moment.

The object of the war of nerves is to misinform, spreading lies among the authorities, in which everyone can participate, thus creating an air of nervousness, discredit, insecurity, uncertainty, and concern on the part of the government.

The best methods used by the urban guerrilla in the war of nerves are the following:

a) using the telephone and the mail to announce false clues to the police and the government, including information on the planting of bombs and any other act of terrorism in public offices and other places, kidnapping and assassination plans, etc., to oblige the authorities to wear themselves out, following up the information fed them;

b) letting false plans fall into the hands of the police to divert their attention;

c) planting rumors to make the government uneasy;

d) exploiting by every means possible the corruption, the errors, and failures of the government and its representatives, forcing them into demoralizing explanations and justifications in the very mass communication media they maintain under censorship;

e) presenting denunciations to foreign embassies, the United Nations, the papal nunciature, and the international judicial commissions defending human rights or freedom of the press, exposing each concrete violation and use of violence by the military dictatorship and making it known that the revolutionary war will continue its course with serious danger for the enemies of the people.

How to Carry Out the Action

The urban guerrilla who correctly carries through his apprenticeship and training must give the greatest importance to his method of carrying out action, for in this he cannot commit the slightest error.

Any carelessness in the assimilation of the method and its use invites certain disaster, as experience teaches every day.

The outlaws commit errors frequently because of their methods, and this is one of the reasons why the urban guerrilla must be so insistently preoccupied with following the revolutionary technique and not the technique of the bandits.

And not only for that reason. There is no urban guerrilla worthy of the name who ignores the revolutionary method of action and fails to practice it rigorously in the planning and execution of his activity.

The giant is known by his toe. The same can be said of the urban

guerrilla who is known from afar for his correct methods and his absolute fidelity to principles.

The revolutionary method of carrying out action is strongly and
forcefully based on the knowledge and use of the following elements:

a) investigation of information;

b) observation or *paquera*;[5]

c) reconnaissance or exploration of the terrain;

d) study and timing of routes;

e) mapping;

f) mechanization;

g) selection of personnel and relief;

h) selection of firing capacity;

i) study and practice in completion;

j) completion;

k) cover;

l) retreat;

m) dispersal;

n) liberation or transfer of prisoners;

o) elimination of clues;

p) rescue of wounded.

Some Observations on the Method

When there is no information, the point of departure for the planning
of the action must be investigation, observation, or *paquera*. This method
also has good results.

In any event, including when there is information, it is essential to
take observations or *paquera*, to see that the information is not at odds
with observation or vice versa.

Reconnaissance or exploration of the terrain, study and timing of
routes are so important that to omit them is to make a stab in the dark.

Mechanization, in general, is an underestimated factor in the method
of conducting the action. Frequently mechanization is left to the end,
to the eve of the action, before anything is done about it.

This is an error. Mechanization must be considered seriously, must
be undertaken with considerable foresight and according to careful
planning, also based on information, observation, or *paquera*, and must
be carried out with rigorous care and precision. The care, conservation,
maintenance, and camouflaging of the vehicles expropriated are very
important details of mechanization.

When transport fails, the principal action fails with serious moral and material consequences for the urban guerrilla activity.

The selection of personnel requires great care to avoid the inclusion of indecisive or vacillating personnel with the danger of contaminating the other participants, a difficulty that must be avoided.

The withdrawal is equally or more important than the operation itself, to the point that it must be rigorously planned, including the possibility of failure.

One must avoid rescue or transfer of prisoners with children present, or anything to attract the attention of people in casual transit through the area. The best thing is to make the rescue as natural as possible, always winding through, or using different routes or narrow streets that scarcely permit passage on foot, to avoid an encounter of two cars. The elimination of tracks is obligatory and demands the greatest caution in hiding fingerprints and any other sign that could give the enemy information. Lack of care in the elimination of tracks and clues is a factor that increases nervousness in our ranks and which the enemy often exploits.

Rescue of the Wounded

The problem of the wounded in urban guerrilla warfare merits special attention. During guerrilla operations in the urban area it may happen that some comrade is accidentally wounded or shot by the police. When a guerrilla in the firing group has a knowledge of first aid he can do something for the wounded comrade on the spot. In no circumstances can the wounded urban guerrilla be abandoned at the site of the battle or left to the enemy's hands.

One of the precautions we must take is to set up nursing courses for men and women, courses in which the urban guerrilla can matriculate and learn the elementary techniques of first aid.

The urban guerrilla doctor, student of medicine, nurse, pharmacologist, or simply the person trained in first aid, is a necessity in modern revolutionary struggle.

A small manual of first aid for the urban guerrilla, printed on mimeographed sheets, can also be undertaken by anyone who has enough knowledge.

In planning and completing an armed action, the urban guerrilla cannot forget the organization of medical logistics. This will be accomplished by means of a mobile or motorized clinic. You can also set up a mobile first aid station. Another solution is to utilize the skills of a nursing comrade who waits with his bag of equipment in a designated house to which the wounded are brought.

The ideal would be to have our own well equipped clinic, but this is very costly unless we use expropriated materials.

When all else fails, it is often necessary to resort to legal clinics, using armed force if necessary to demand that the doctors attend to our wounded.

In the eventuality that we fall back on blood banks to buy blood or whole plasma, we must not use legal addresses and certainly not addresses where the wounded can really be found, since they are under our care and protection. Nor should we supply addresses of those involved in the organization's clandestine work to the hospitals and health centers where we take them. Such concerns are indispensable to cover any track or clue.

The houses in which the wounded stay cannot be known to anybody with the unique and exclusive exception of the small group of comrades responsible for their treatment and transport.

Sheets, bloody clothing, medicine, and any other indication of treatment of the comrades wounded in combat with the police, must be completely eliminated from any place they visit to receive medical treatment.

Guerrilla Security

The urban guerrilla lives in constant danger of the possibility of being discovered or denounced. The chief security problem is to make certain that we are well hidden and well guarded, and that there are secure methods to keep the police from locating us or our whereabouts.

The worst enemy of the urban guerrilla and the major danger we run is infiltration into our organization by a spy or an informer.

The spy trapped within the organization will be punished with death. The same goes for those who desert and inform the police.

A good security is the certainty that the enemy has no spies and agents infiltrated in our midst and can receive no information about us even by indirect or distant means. The fundamental way to insure this is to be cautious and strict in recruiting.

Nor is it permissible for everyone to know everyone and everything else. Each person should know only what relates to his work. This rule is a fundamental point in the abc's of urban guerrilla security.

The battle that we are waging against the enemy is arduous and difficult because it is a class struggle. Every class struggle is a battle of life or death when the classes are antagonistic.

The enemy wants to annihilate us and fights relentlessly to find us and destroy us, so that our great weapon consists in hiding from him and attacking him by surprise.

The danger to the urban guerrilla is that he may reveal himself through imprudence or allow himself to be discovered through lack of class vigilance. It is inadmissible for the urban guerrilla to give out his own or any other clandestine address to the enemy or to talk too much. Annotations in the margins of newspapers, lost documents, calling cards, letters or notes, all these are clues that the police never underestimate.

Address and telephone books must be destroyed and one must not write or hold papers; it is necessary to avoid keeping archives of legal or illegal names, biographical information, maps, and plans. The points of contact should not be written down but simply committed to memory.

The urban guerrilla who violates these rules must be warned by the first one who notes his infraction and, if he repeats it, we must avoid working with him.

The need of the urban guerrilla to move about constantly and the relative proximity of the police, given the circumstances of the strategic police net which surrounds the city, forces him to adopt variable security methods depending on the enemy's movements.

For this reason it is necessary to maintain a service of daily news about what the enemy appears to be doing, where his police net is operating and what gorges and points of strangulation are being watched. The daily reading of police news in the newspapers is a great fountain of information in these cases.

The most important lesson for guerrilla security is never, under any circumstances, to permit the slightest sign of laxity in the maintenance of security measures and regulations within the organization.

Guerrilla security must be maintained also and principally in cases of arrest. The arrested guerrilla can reveal nothing to the police that will jeopardize the organization. He can say nothing that may lead, as a consequence, to the arrest of other comrades, the discovery of addresses and hiding places, the loss of arms and ammunition.

The Seven Sins of the Urban Guerrilla

Even when the urban guerrilla applies his revolutionary technique with precision and rigorously abides by security rules, he can still be vulnerable to errors. There is no perfect urban guerrilla. The most he can do is to make every effort to diminish the margin of error since he cannot be perfect.

One of the methods we should use to diminish the margin of error is to know thoroughly the seven sins of the urban guerrilla and try to fight them.

The first sin of the urban guerrilla is inexperience. The urban guerrilla, blinded by this sin, thinks the enemy is stupid, underestimates his intelligence, believes everything is easy and, as a result, leaves clues that can lead to his disaster.

Because of his inexperience, the urban guerrilla can also overestimate the forces of the enemy, believing them to be stronger than they really are. Allowing himself to be fooled by this presumption, the urban guerrilla becomes intimidated, and remains insecure and indecisive, paralyzed and lacking in audacity.

The second sin of the urban guerrilla is to boast about the actions he has completed and broadcast them to the four winds.

The third sin of the urban guerrilla is vanity. The urban guerrilla who suffers from this sin tries to solve the problems of the revolution by actions erupting in the city, but without bothering about the beginnings and the survival of the guerrilla in rural areas. Blinded by success, he winds up organizing an action that he considers decisive and that puts into play all the forces and resources of the organization. Since the city is the area of the strategic circle which we cannot avoid or break while rural guerrilla warfare has not yet erupted and is not at the point of triumph, we always run the fatal error of permitting the enemy to attack us with decisive blows.

The fourth sin of the urban guerrilla is to exaggerate his strength and to undertake projects for which he lacks forces and, as yet, does not have the required infrastructure.

The fifth sin of the urban guerrilla is precipitous action. The urban guerrilla who commits this sin loses patience, suffers an attack of nerves, does not wait for anything, and impetuously throws himself into action, suffering untold reverses.

The sixth sin of the urban guerrilla is to attack the enemy when he is most angry.

The seventh sin of the urban guerrilla is to fail to plan things and to act out of improvisation.

Popular Support

One of the permanent concerns of the urban guerrilla is his identification with popular causes to win public support.

Where government actions become inept and corrupt, the urban guerrilla should not hesitate to step in to show that he opposes the government and to gain mass sympathy. The present government, for example, imposes heavy financial burdens and excessively high taxes on the people. It is up to the urban guerrilla to attack the dictatorship's tax collection system and to obstruct its financial activity, throwing all the weight of violent revolutionary action against it.

The urban guerrilla fights not only to upset the tax and collection system: the arm of revolutionary violence must also be directed against those government organs that raise prices and those who direct them, as well as against the wealthiest of the national and foreign profiteers and the important property owners; in short, against all those who accumulate huge fortunes out of the high cost of living, the wages of hunger, excessive prices and rents.

Foreign trusts, such as refrigeration and other North American plants that monopolize the market and the manufacture of general food supplies, must be systematically attacked by the urban guerrilla.

The rebellion of the urban guerrilla and his persistence in intervening in public questions is the best way of insuring public support of the cause we defend. We repeat and insist on repeating: *it is the best way of insuring public support.* As soon as a reasonable section of the population begins to take seriously the action of the urban guerrilla, his success is guaranteed.

The government has no alternative except to intensify repression. The police networks, house searches, arrests of innocent people and of suspects, closing off streets, make life in the city unbearable. The military dictatorship embarks on massive political persecution. Political assassinations and police terror become routine.

In spite of all this, the police systematically fail. The armed forces, the navy, and the air force are mobilized and undertake routine police functions. Even so they find no way to halt guerrilla operations, nor to wipe out the revolutionary organization with its fragmented groups that move around and operate throughout the national territory persistently and contagiously.

The people refuse to collaborate with the authorities, and the general sentiment is that the government is unjust, incapable of solving problems, and resorts purely and simply to the physical liquidation of its opponents.

The political situation in the country is transformed into a military situation in which the gorillas appear more and more to be the ones responsible for errors and violence, while the problems in the lives of the people become truly catastrophic.

When they see the militarists and the dictatorship on the brink of the abyss and fearing the consequences of a revolutionary war which is already at a fairly advanced and irreversible level, the pacifiers, always to be found within the ruling classes, and the right-wing opportunists, partisans of nonviolent struggle, join hands and circulate rumors behind the scenes, begging the hangmen for elections, "redemocratization," constitutional reforms, and other tripe designed to fool the masses and make them stop the revolutionary rebellion in the cities and the rural areas of the country.

But, watching the revolutionaries, the people now understand that it is a farce to vote in elections which have as their sole objective guaranteeing the continuation of the military dictatorship and covering up its crimes.

Attacking wholeheartedly this election farce and the so-called "political solution" so appealing to the opportunists, the urban guerrilla must become more aggressive and violent, resorting without letup to sabotage, terrorism, expropriations, assaults, kidnappings, executions, etc.

This answers any attempt to fool the masses with the opening of Congress and the reorganization of political parties—parties of the government and of the opposition it allows—when all the time the parliament and the so-called parties function thanks to the license of the military dictatorship in a true spectacle of marionettes and dogs on a leash.

The role of the urban guerrilla, in order to win the support of the people, is to continue fighting, keeping in mind the interests of the masses and heightening the disastrous situation in which the government must act. These are the circumstances, disastrous for the dictatorship, which permit the revolutionaries to open rural guerrilla warfare in the midst of the uncontrollable expansion of urban rebellion.

The urban guerrilla is engaged in revolutionary action in favor of the people and with it seeks the participation of the masses in the struggle against the military dictatorship and for the liberation of the country from the yoke of the United States. Beginning with the city and with the support of the people, the rural guerrilla war develops rapidly, establishing its infrastructure carefully while the urban area continues the rebellion.

Urban Guerrilla Warfare, School for Selecting the Guerrilla

Revolution is a social phenomenon that depends on men, arms, and resources. Arms and resources exist in the country and can be taken and used, but to do this it is necessary to count on men. Without them, the arms and the resources have no use and no value. For their part, the men must have two basic and indispensable obligatory qualities:

a) they must have a politico-revolutionary motivation;

b) they must have the necessary technical-revolutionary preparation.

Men with a politico-revolutionary motivation are found among the vast and clearheaded contingents of enemies of the military dictatorship and of the domination of U.S. imperialism.

Almost daily such men gravitate to urban guerrilla warfare, and it is for this reason that the reaction no longer announces that it has thwarted the revolutionaries and goes through the unpleasantness of seeing them rise up again out of their own ashes.

The men who are best trained, most experienced, and dedicated to urban guerrilla warfare and at the same time to rural guerrilla warfare, constitute the backbone of the revolutionary war and, therefore, of the Brazilian revolution. From this backbone will come the marrow of the revolutionary army of national liberation, rising out of guerrilla warfare.

This is the central nucleus, not the bureaucrats and opportunists hidden in the organizational structure, not the empty conferees, the clichéd writers of resolutions that remain on paper, but rather the men who fight. The men who from the very first have been determined and ready for anything, who personally participate in revolutionary actions, who do not waver or deceive.

This is the nucleus indoctrinated and disciplined with a long-range strategic and tactical vision consistent with the application of Marxist theory, of Leninism, and of Castro-Guevara developments applied to the specific conditions of the Brazilian situation. This is the nucleus that will lead the rebellion through its guerrilla phase.

From it will come men and women with politico-military development, one and indivisible, whose task will be that of future leaders after the triumph of the revolution, in the construction of the new Brazilian society.

As of now, the men and women chosen for urban guerrilla warfare are workers; peasants whom the city has attracted as a market for manpower and who return to the countryside indoctrinated and politically and technically prepared: students, intellectuals, priests. This is the material with which we are building—starting with urban guerrilla warfare —the armed alliance of workers and peasants, with students, intellectuals, priests.

Workers have infinite knowledge in the industrial sphere and are best for urban revolutionary tasks. The urban guerrilla worker participates in the struggle by constructing arms, sabotaging and preparing saboteurs and dynamiters, and personally participating in actions involving hand arms, or organizing strikes and partial paralysis with the characteristics of mass violence in factories, workships, and other work centers.

The peasants have an extraordinary intuition for knowledge of the land, judgment in confronting the enemy, and the indispensable ability to communicate with the humble masses. The peasant guerrilla is already participating in our struggle and it is he who reaches the guerrilla core, establishes support points in the countryside, finds hiding places for individuals, arms, munitions, supplies, organizes the sowing and harvesting of grain for use in the guerrilla war, chooses the points of transport, cattle-raising posts, and sources of meat supplies, trains the guides that show the rural guerrillas the road, and creates an information service in the countryside.

Students are noted for being politically crude and coarse and thus they break all the taboos. When they are integrated into urban guerrilla warfare, as is now occurring on a wide scale, they show a special talent for revolutionary violence and soon acquire a high level of political-technical-military skill. Students have plenty of free time on their hands because they are systematically separated, suspended, and expelled from school by the dictatorship and so they begin to spend their time advantageously, in behalf of the revolution.

The intellectuals constitute the vanguard of resistance to arbitrary acts, social injustice, and the terrible inhumanity of the dictatorship of the gorillas. They spread the revolutionary call and they have great influence on people. The urban guerrilla intellectual or artist is the most modern of the Brazilian revolution's adherents.

Churchmen—that is to say, those ministers or priests and religious men of various hierarchies and persuasions—represent a sector that has special ability to communicate with the people, particularly with workers, peasants, and the Brazilian woman. The priest who is an urban guerrilla is an active ingredient in the ongoing Brazilian revolutionary war, and constitutes a powerful arm in the struggle against military power and North American imperialism.

As for the Brazilian woman, her participation in the revolutionary war, and particularly in urban guerrilla warfare, has been marked by an unmatched fighting spirit and tenacity, and it is not by chance that so many women have been accused of participation in guerrilla actions against banks, quarries, military centers, etc., and that so many are in prison while others are sought by the police.

As a school for choosing the guerrilla, urban guerrilla warfare prepares and places at the same level of responsibility and efficiency the men and women who share the same dangers fighting, rounding up supplies, serving as messengers or runners, as drivers, sailors, or airplane pilots, obtaining secret information, and helping with propaganda and the task of indoctrination.

Carlos Marighella

June 1969

ONE HUNDRED FIFTY QUESTIONS TO A GUERRILLA 6

by Alberto Bayo Giroud

One of the first detailed and instructive works on the conduct of guerrilla and urban warfare was Alberto Bayo Giroud's *150 Questions to a Guerrilla*. Bayo, an officer in the Spanish army, garnered extensive knowledge of guerrilla warfare while fighting the Moors and Riffs in Africa. He later fought in the Spanish Civil War, and afterwards, having settled in Mexico, he involved himself in training groups of Latin American revolutionists. It was due to these activities that he was approached by a Cuban exile named Fidel Castro Ruz and asked to train an expeditionary group that Castro planned to lead into Cuba.

Bayo prepared Castro and his followers, and the rebels set out for Cuba on 25 November 1956. The rest is history. Bayo did not accompany the expeditionaries, but he did resume contact with Castro after the rebels had established themselves in the mountains of eastern Cuba. Displaying full understanding of the value to a revolutionary movement of engaging in terrorist activities, Bayo wrote to Castro:

> Start activating a program of agitation on a large scale to encompass the most important cities. Begin with your active groups to terrorize the population, using bombs, petards, Molotov cocktails, lighted matches in public vehicles, etc. If this fails, or if you see that the people don't respond, begin a wave of sabotage aimed in particular against the sugar centers of the interior. If this also fails, then start with personal attempts on the lives of individuals belonging to the armed forces and the police.[1]

Once the rebels were victorious in Cuba, Bayo returned to that country (he had been born in Cuba and had taught there after the Spanish

Civil War). He was honored by the new Castro regime for the assistance
he had rendered. Among the Castro followers whom Bayo had trained in
Mexico was an Argentine wanderer named Ernesto Guevara de la Serna,
and it was Guevara that Bayo considered to be his best pupil. After the
Cuban Revolution, which saw Guevara develop into one of the important guerrilla leaders of our times, Guevara acknowledged that Bayo
was "my teacher."[2] Bayo's capability as a teacher was fully utilized by
the Castro government in its efforts—directed by Guevara—to extend
revolutionary activities to other Latin American countries. He helped
train groups of Latin Americans who then went back to carry out guerrilla and urban warfare campaigns in their homelands.

Bayo's *150 Questions to a Guerrilla* was used as a textbook in training
the prospective guerrillas. The book was first published in Mexico, possibly in 1955. Following the Castro victory, a substantial number of
editions were printed and distributed among would-be revolutionaries
throughout the hemisphere. Usually these copies of the book were small
in size, fitting easily into the pockets of guerrillas.

The work is unique among its kind in that it is in the form of questions and answers. In addition to text, some editions also contain drawings explaining such things as how to make simple bombs, bangalore
torpedoes, and incendiary devices; how to set booby traps, how to stop
cars, and how to blow up tanks, trains, and bridges.

150 Questions is of note because it contains more than simple instructions on the techniques and equipment of guerrilla and urban warfare.
The directions are there, in great detail, but underlying all that Bayo says
is his emphasis on the need of rebels to be supported by the populace, to
be identified with the people of the land in which they seek to operate.
In the answer to his first question Bayo states that rebels must engage in
a "struggle against the injustices which a people suffer." He warns,
"Whoever revolts unrighteously reaps nothing but a crushing defeat."

Bayo repeatedly asserts that rebels must win and maintain good relations with peasants and city folk. He urges that food taken from peasants "be paid for at a good price," and that the peasants be assisted in
their farm tasks in order to "attract [them] to our cause so that we may
eventually request their help at any time." If rebels need houses in a
town, "we will try to convince [the inhabitants] gently that they must
evacuate their houses . . ."

Even an automobile accident can be utilized against the government,
if one of the drivers happens to be a government driver. In this case,
Bayo advises, "direct the indignation of the people against him."

Bayo misses few opportunities for trouble and mischief.

ONE HUNDRED FIFTY QUESTIONS TO A GUERRILLA

1. *In order for a guerrilla war to succeed, exactly what preconditions should exist?*

To BE right in your struggle against the injustices which a people suffer, whether from foreign invasion, the imposition of a dictatorship, the existence of a government which is an enemy to the people, an oligarchic regime, etc. If these conditions do not exist, the guerrilla war will always be defeated. Whoever revolts unrighteously reaps nothing but a crushing defeat.

2. *Who should take part in a guerrilla unit?*
— Primarily only young men and women who are firm in their convictions, cautious in their dealings, have proven their spirit of self-sacrifice, personal courage, patriotism, and great dedication to the cause of the people should take part in a guerrilla war.

3. *In addition to these moral qualifications what else must one who intends to join our guerrilla organization do?*
— He must truthfully and in detail answer questions on a questionnaire which includes such information as the applicant's full name; place and date of birth; marital status; names of parents; names of spouse, children, etc.; places of work since the age of eighteen; names of friends in the Revolutionary Movement; whether he has ever been arrested; and many other questions which our Movement has worked out. The applicant must give a history of his political position. After completion of the questionnaire and our obtaining a favorable impression from the investigation of the data supplied, he will be admitted to the appropriate guerrilla unit.

4. *If the results of the investigation of his questionnaire reveal the applicant to be an informer or spy who intends to enter our ranks to betray us, what shall we do with him?*
— He will be judged by the Summary Court Martial as a traitor to the revolution.

5. *If in spite of all steps we take, a despicable spy infiltrates the organization, what shall we do with him?*
— Once his status has been verified as such, he will be judged by Court Martial and without pity sentenced to death. We can pardon a political enemy who fights for an ideal which in our estimation is wrong, but never

a spy. Such a man deserves no consideration even though to the enemy he may be a hero or martyr. The accused should be given every right which his situation warrants, especially since he may really be an agent working for us who was ordered by his supervisors to engage in counterespionage.

6. *How many guerrillas work in a guerrilla unit?*
— The ideal number is between ten and twenty. The fewer the men, the greater the mobility.

7. *How fast does a guerrilla unit make an amphibious landing and how is it achieved?*
— The unit is only as fast as the slowest of its members. To effect a landing everything must be planned and rehearsed in advance so that as soon as the unit hits the beach every member moves quickly, silently, well disciplined and well briefed in his particular task. Those who are assigned to take the hills commanding the beach move off to the left flank; those who are to take and hold the center run forward and assume their positions, then rapidly unload the material from the boat as quickly as possible, maintaining discipline and absolute silence as though they were a group of deaf mutes, not even being able to signal to one another.

8. *What is done with guerrillas who cannot withstand long marches?*
— They are brought together to form slower units within which, however, everyone has to keep up.

9. *Who should captain a guerrilla unit?*
— The captain should be the one who because of his special qualifications of command ability, character, intelligence, caution, zest for combat, etc. is nominated for the position.

10. *Should a guerrilla be informed of the higher command organization?*
— Yes, he should know it and abide by it so that when there are casualties there will be no disagreement as to who is to command a unit. Vacated positions are taken over by the person with the next highest authority and who will be respected and obeyed by all subordinates.

11. *What weapons should a guerrilla unit carry?*
— The unit should be equipped with the same type of rifles to facilitate the supply of ammunition, and in addition, it is good to have a light machine gun which is always useful in our operations. Each guerrilla should

always carry his own first-aid kit, canteen, a watch synchronized with the unit leader's, and many need field glasses. A guerrilla should also wear as a belt a rope some six feet long which can be used at night by a companion who holds on to one end thus not losing contact with his unit. This "tail" is worn wound around the waist. The part left over is what his companion, following behind, holds on to. No one is ever lost this way, no matter how dark the night is. It can be used in scaling peaks, crossing rivers, and for tying up bundles of firewood.

12. *How should the guerrilla unit be equipped?*
— Its men should have good heavy shoes with thick soles and count on one good compass per unit. These are indispensable. Maps of the sector should always be available in order not to have to ask directions of any peasant. But if necessary he should only be used to confirm data already on the map.

13. *How should a guerrilla unit be organized?*
— Exactly like an army corps, with its staff, its different positions and responsibilities filled by guerrillas so all the work does not fall on one man. Therefore the guerrilla unit is composed of the following sections: intelligence, operations, sabotage, recruiting, training, armament, munitions, quartermaster, sanitation, and propaganda.

14. *What are the duties of each of these sections?*
— Intelligence should compile all the information it can on all members of the guerrilla unit, all enemies, those indifferent to the movement; on the location of water, springs and rivers; on roads, highways, trails, bridges; on the conduct of the guerrilla members; on sympathizers who wish to join the unit; on soldiers, informers, spies, etc. At the same time it will obtain or make maps of the terrain and the principal targets in the sector assigned to the unit. It will conduct espionage and counterespionage activities, keep records on unit personnel regarding all combat performance whether outstanding or unimpressive; and carry on cryptographic work (coding and deciphering messages, documents of courts martial, etc.).

The Intelligence Section should be under the direction of the second in command of the guerrilla unit, who should himself possess a high degree of intelligence, wisdom, and caution.

The Operations Section will supervise all attacks and other missions the unit undertakes and will evaluate the results of these endeavors. It consults with the comrades responsible for carrying out the missions, keeps the commander posted on the development of projects so he can make the final decision as to whether the operation will be put into effect. When the captain is unable to command a unit because of wounds, severe illness, or necessary absence, the head of Operations takes over his command, filing all data required for operations, both proposed and ready for accomplishment, along with different scale maps of the sector.

Leadership of the Sabotage Section, the main one of the ten composing our staff, falls to an active officer, extraordinarily dynamic, extremely intelligent and clever, having a creative imagination, adaptability, and a real vocation for his assignment. He must conduct his missions so that all types of sabotage are exploited to the fullest; if possible hitting new objectives daily.

The Recruiting Section obtains personnel to fill out our ranks or replace our losses. It will list names of young volunteers separating them into three groups. In the first group will be those who are to replace our casualties; in the second, those who can serve as machete men or demolition agents; and the third group, used only for the construction of fortifications and other such tasks.

The officer in charge of training will supervise the training in handling firearms and close order drill, literacy courses for peasants, and all educational and cultural programs of the guerrilla unit.

The Armament Section is concerned with the maintenance of the unit's weapons; with the shotguns of the shotgunners serving with our forces as well as with our hand guns.

It will keep lists of instructors and armorers and their assistants, providing for the acquisition of replacement parts needed to maintain our arms in good repair.

The Munitions Section is in charge of everything pertaining to the guerrilla unit's ammunition. It trains civilians who are to pass cartridges on to the guerrillas, and furthermore maintains small caches of cartridges and spare parts so that in no encounter will the guerrilla be without munitions.

The Quartermaster Section, because of its vital importance, will be the province of one of the most responsible men in the unit. This section sees to it that food is never lacking for the troop, rationing intelligently whatever it has, and assuring by its negotiations, orders, and purchases the feeding of the unit.

The Sanitation chief doesn't have to be a doctor or nurse, although it would be helpful if he were. This section has the responsibility for keeping a complete stock of medicine, and whatever else is needed to bring our comrades back to health. This includes the addresses of doctors and nurses in our sector who will either voluntarily treat our men or who will be forced to do so when called upon.

The man in charge of Propaganda will make known all our successful exploits in newspapers and magazines throughout the country; and if that is not possible, then by means of letters, mimeographed bulletins, etc. This publicizing of our military accomplishments will raise the morale of our people and wear down the morale of our enemies.

In Combat

15. *What physical training should a guerrilla have before going on missions?*
— He will engage in even longer marches until reaching a total of fifteen hours duration with only a short rest of ten minutes every four hours; besides, he will practice night marches of seven hours, at least.

16. *How should one move about in the field at night?*
— One should walk as though riding a bicycle, lifting the feet high each step in order not to trip over stones, tree trunks, or other objects in your way. Use your compass at least every hour to check your directions. If you have no compass you can orient yourself by the polar star whose location you will learn in our manuals. On starless nights you can get your bearings from the trees. In our countries, the north side of live trees has either no bark or the bark is thin and worn.

17. *How should guerrillas treat one another?*
— Everyone should be friendly or at least cooperative. Practical jokes and tricks are considered bad taste. They cause enmity among the men, weaken the unit's strength, and therefore are forbidden in our organization.

18. *How can one orient himself during the day?*
— By means of the sun. Stand pointing your right arm and side toward the place the sun has risen. This arm points toward the east; the opposite side is the west; in front of you, north; and at your back, south.

19. *When in the field we come upon a house or peasant's hut, how should we proceed before entering for the first time?*
— Only two of our number will go in; the others will let the occupants of

the building know they are surrounded in case they are enemies or intend to betray us. When a careful search of the house has been made and the possibilities of betrayal or the hiding of enemies in the house have been ruled out, the rest of the guerrilla unit can enter after lookouts have been placed on the hills overlooking the road along which enemies might come. While we are inside, we will not let anyone leave, for he might warn an enemy. The recruiting officer will be in charge of interrogating the owner and discerning his true feeling toward us. Afterwards he will be asked to help as an informal agent, or as a farm guerrilla. If he refuses, showing open sympathy for the enemy cause, he will be made to leave the area; for it is impossible in an area where the guerrilla unit is operating to allow freedom of movement to individuals who might be working against us. Once he has been told to leave his house or farm we will attach all of his property without any compensation. All his belongings will become the property of the armed forces of popular liberation.

20. *What shall we do with the young men who wish to join our unit?* — The recruiting section will process them one by one, investigating their merits and deciding whether we can accept them as fellow-soldiers in our revolutionary struggle. In case we can, they are trained to be farm guerrillas; if we have the weapons and the need for more people, they can be taken in as regular guerrillas after receiving the proper training. I personally trained Calixto Sánchez's guerrilla leaders who later landed in Oriente, and in Cabonico, and whose initial operation was a complete success. Not a cartridge was lost; only one boat, which got stuck on the beach. Many times in my classes I emphasized that those who did not voluntarily offer to join up might be accepted one at a time, searched, and given a rigorous interrogation by the recruiting officer to decide who should be assigned to our elite, to the regulars (the less inspired), or to the third section—the unreliables. But we never accept people merely because they claim to be on our side. Calixto Sánchez's leaders did not follow this warning, one which I learned well in a hundred encounters with the enemy. When a group of soldiers dressed as peasants came up shouting, "Viva Fidel Castro!", our people received them with open arms. The soldiers then drew their pistols from hiding and arrested our men saying they were surrounded by many others in the mountains. Our guerrillas, new at the tricks of war, were stricken by fear, the disease that all unseasoned troops are subject to. The rest is well known. They were taken prisoners and that butcher Colonel Cowley assassinated all that were with Calixto Sánchez. Cowley, in turn, was later brought down by a heroic

shotgunner of the 26th of July Movement. Only the seven men in Calixto Sánchez' advanced guard, commanded by Héctor Cornillot, survived this encounter and later most of them joined the Sierra Maestra units.

21. *What should the guerrilla unit do after an amphibious landing?*
— Once on the beach, we march toward the highest ridge offering concealment. Of course this is after hiding in the most appropriate places all the heavy materiel we have unloaded. If we succeed in moving inland in secrecy, we carry along our materiel to hide in even safer places in the highlands.

22. *Can you tell me some of the assignments in which volunteers of both sexes can assist?*
— Here are some of the missions they can undertake:
   1. To form a small platoon of attendants for each guerrilla unit.
   2. To provide pairs of people to serve as scouts in front and on the flanks.
   3. To provide liaison pairs to give proper personnel status reports to the command post.
   4. To act as runners to maintain contact with the flanks.
   5. To provide large platoons to comb (clean) the enemies from our zone of control. This job must be done frequently.
   6. Other platoons can ask the loan of hammers, nails, saws, picks, shovels, hoes, barbed wire, food, canteens, empty bottles and tin cans, and typewriters that the commander requires.
   7. Others may compile a list of volunteers, both men and women, of the proper age to give service.
   8. To form political groups to inquire of the political leanings of the people in our zone.
   9. To select individuals who are ready and able to make our status reports, plans, selected scale maps, detailed operational information, to keep guerrilla service records, speeches to the people, etc.
   10. Printers, typists, mimeographists, and others may work in the propaganda section.
   11. To form brigades of propagandists of our revolutionary ideas to carry out meetings in plazas and other places.
   12. To form police platoons, in which women should participate, to impose order and to prevent robbery, pillage, violations, and abuses.
   13. To provide and guard storage for our material.
   14. Women will also be used to bring complete information from

cities not yet dominated by us. By sending many of them to the same place without their knowing that they have the same mission, more complete and cross-checked information will be gained.

15. To form water carriers and quartermaster personnel and distributers of provisions from the women.

16. Women can be used to form a corps of nurses and helpers.

17. To form the sections of carrier pigeons.

18. To establish a report-carrying section using trained dogs.

19. Cooks.

20. Cook's helpers.

21. Wood carriers for the kitchen.

22. Kitchen dishwashers.

23. Water carriers for the kitchen.

24. Seamstresses.

25. Clothes ironers.

26. Laundresses.

27. Registerers of home residents (preferably women).

28. Bathkeepers.

29. Typists, for consignment to sections that ask for them.

30. Separation, storage, and control of captured enemy clothing.

31. Hospital personnel.

32. To form units of saboteurs of trains, highways, bridges, wire communications, etc.

33. To make groups of slingers and throwers of incendiary bombs.

34. Teams of sling instructors.

35. To provide picked groups designated to prepare incendiary bottles, filling them with gasoline and capping them, so that they will be ready at the proper time.

36. From the most intelligent and brave women, to form sowers of fear.

37. Statisticians.

38. To form a group of carpenters to make sawhorses, barbs, fence stakes, trench floors when the ground is wet, grenade boxes, frames to mount rails in trenches, etc.

39. As groups to collect rails for fortification works.

40. To carry the rails to the place of their use.

41. To form recruiting parties to bring people from villages not yet controlled.

42. To form espionage and counterespionage sections.

43. To make up flag and signal communication sections.

44. For fortification works, using whatever workshops that are available.

45. To provide day and night relief teams.

46. To form cavalry with whatever animals are available among the people.

47. Enemy aircraft spotters.

48. Basket carriers to carry dirt from the trenches.

49. Arms cleaners.

50. Cold steel weapons (cutting weapons) storage.

51. Providers of horse rations.

52. Investigation of traitors.

53. Food storage.

54. Throwers of incendiaries against vehicles on the roads.

55. Personnel to set up and improve airfields.

56. Tree cutters.

57. Keeper of the "operations diary."

58. Correspondents.

59. Letter carriers.

60. Tool keepers.

23. *What is the first offensive action that a recently formed guerrilla unit should take?*

— Our first action, as soon as we reach our sector, is to cut in as many places we can, all roads and railroads so that our enemies will only be able to travel on foot. We must force them into infantry roles. Because of their inferior training, lack of morale, because they are armed forces at the service of the oligarchic enemies of the people, and because of their lack of fighting spirit they should be very inferior to our forces who, with greater nobility and efficiency of personnel, are in better condition than the enemy. We should not become panic-stricken under any circumstances, even though the enemy might throw thousands of men at us. We will have a better chance to inflict casualties on him. It would be more dangerous to our guerrilla team of fifteen men if they assigned twenty-five soldiers to hunt us down. This is worse than having a thousand after us. Always remember that Sandino fought against the Americans for seven years without once being cornered in spite of his pursuers' many thousands of perfectly trained men with motorized units and dozens of radios beaming concentric rings around the Sierra de Segovia where our hero was fighting. After seven years of fruitless pursuit they had to grant him a truce on his own terms. Augusto César Sandino, the Nicaraguan patriot, was assassinated a short time after leaving the Segovia highlands.

24. *What should we do with the peasants who wish to join us?*
— The recruiting officer will organize them into two different divisions. Into the first one will be put fighting men whom we trust completely, and into the second will go those who can be utilized on secondary combat tasks such as water carriers, wood cutters for the mess units, and porters for long marches. To those individuals who display an avid desire for combat and have unquestionable backgrounds will be issued machetes and incendiary bombs. They will march along with our unit as members of machete and bomb squads.

25. *When should we do battle with the enemy?*
— This is the prime question for a guerrilla unit. The answer should be learned by heart and always put into practice. The perfect guerrilla, that is the one who best serves the daily interests of the peoples revolutionary cause, is one who never invites the enemy to do battle. Nor does he accept challenge to fight the enemy who hopes to meet us where he would hold the advantage. Every good guerrilla should attack by surprise, in skirmishes and ambushes, and when the enemy least suspects any action. When the soldiers load and prepare to repel our attack, we should all fade out of sight and redeploy in safer places. Obviously, in all actions we try to inflict the heaviest possible casualties. We will never lose visual contact with our enemies; that is, we will accompany them from afar keeping within field glass range so that we are constantly aware of their position. If we do not fire into their quarters every night we are not performing our duty as guerrillas. A good guerrilla is one who looks after his men not exposing them to enemy fire; he makes sure they cannot see his troops with camouflage and skillful tactics. He hounds the enemy day and night, carrying on "minuet" tactics. That is, he advances when the enemy falls back; retreating to our right when the enemy plans to encircle us on that flank. We always keep the same distance from the enemy forces: some 800 to a thousand yards by day, sending two or three of our sharpshooters up as close as possible during the night to pester them, and thus bringing about the highest number of casualties.

26. *How should a police headquarters be attacked?*
— If the headquarters is built in the center of a lot one hundred yards wide by fifty in length, there will be fifty yards between the building and the fence surrounding it.

First, we have to take the adjacent buildings and with our fire force the garrison to take cover, waiting for reinforcements and outside help. Once in possession of a neighboring building and setting our riflemen around the headquarters so that no one can escape, we will begin our plan of attack as follows: In the building we have taken, we will dig a tunnel toward the center of the headquarters. Once we have the first shaft and the tunnel begun, we put two men with pick axes shoulder to shoulder digging a six-foot-high tunnel. Each one digs out a cubic yard of earth. They then withdraw while the dirt is quickly removed by others with shovels and baskets. When one side of the tunnel is clear of loose dirt, the shovel and basket men withdraw and the pick men begin again. All the workers thus have a break and can perform their tasks with greater efficiency. The tunnel bores away underground, just wide enough to allow two to work without interference. All work as fast as possible; the supervisor relieves the men when they seem to be slowing down.

It is next to impossible for reinforcements to reach the garrison by day so it will probably surrender. If it does not do so soon, it should be blown up—first with the object of taking it over; secondly, as a lesson for other police hedaquarters to surrender quickly. To hasten the job, not only one tunnel will be dug, but many leading under the headquarters. We do not know what kind of earth we will encounter in any one tunnel, nor whether the first mining attempt will be successful. A second or third bombing may be needed.

If on igniting the charge we discover that the blast is not underneath the building, our soldiers, ready and waiting, should be sent into the tunnel to reach the garrison from the crater or at least to occupy the crater. It has to be somewhere near the building and as such serve as a good place to attack the building from.

For these operations we need the following teams: strong men for the picks, shovelmen, and basketmen; those to handle the lanterns and other tunnel lights; those who will shore up the tunnel after it is dug; and finally those who will set the charge, as well as soldiers to race down the tunnel after the explosion.

Before setting off one tunnel explosion under the headquarters, all other tunnel activities from other buildings must be halted so as to safeguard our comrades.

We have to be prepared at all times for a counterattack from the garrison itself as well as by the army, keeping a 24-hour guard posted. We also will make beforehand the necessary preparations for accommodating the wounded, prisoners, and the dead resulting from the attack. One man will be assigned to take care of all equipment we might capture. All enemy survivors will be given a thorough interrogation to learn what should be done with them.

If, after the first explosion the garrison still does not surrender, we keep up work intensively on the other tunnels as well as in the first one. After an unsuccessful first attempt we should be able to correct the angle for the next try. Up to the time of the second bomb, the first crater can be used to pin down the occupants of the building from close by.

After the headquarters has been taken, the teams we have utilized in the tunnel operations will be sent on to other targets to do similar work.

When all garrisons in our zone have fallen, these specialists will be given jobs in our corps of engineers. The leaders of tunneling operations will at all times inform the general staff of their progress.

As a closing note to this section keep in mind that from all of the world's famous prisons, men have escaped by digging their way under walls and past sentinels.

27. *What should be done before attacking from a tunnel?*
— If it is not possible to achieve a surprise attack, an intense psychological campaign should be carried out making use of emissaries, wives of the besieged, local bigwigs, and enemy prisoners taken in previous attacks.

28. *How is a guerrilla column on the march made up?*
— The guerrillas cover their flanks (right and left sides), an advance party (those preceding the main body) and rear guard (protecting from behind) utilizing peasants who volunteer (as they all should) to help us, as well as troops from the guerrilla unit itself.

29. *What should appear on service records?*
— The dates and places where each guerrilla has fought in addition to his rating as a soldier in each action, and whether he received any distinction for his performance. It is important to be precise in keeping service records so that promotions can be given to the most valuable men.

30. *How can you make a hand grenade?*
— Take an empty condensed milk can, dry it thoroughly inside; put in a dynamite cap, nails or small pieces of iron; press smoothly so no sparks are produced; be careful not to jar or hit it. Continue inserting other dynamite caps and more shrapnel, tamping gently each time until the can is full. A wooden or metal cover is then placed over the can after the contents have been compressed as much as possible. The cover should be pierced to allow a fuse with a percussion cap at its end to make contact

with the dynamite. On lighting the fuse, the percussion cap is exploded, which in turn ignites the dynamite in the grenade.

31. *How can you make a land mine?*
— Take a length of pipe, seal it at one end by welding or screwing on a pipe cap. Fill it with dynamite and cover the open end, leaving a small hole in the cap for the fuse. Insert a tube about ⅛ of an inch thick with a percussion cap in the end contacting the dynamite. In the other end of the fuse, place a wad of cotton impregnated with potassium chlorate and sugar. Another wad of cotton, and next to this a little glass chamber containing sulfuric acid are next inserted into the fuse tube, making certain the glass receptacle is well-sealed to keep the acid inside. Next, stick in a length of metal or wood for a plunger that can slide easily down the tube to break the glass. This releases the acid which forms a chemical reaction with the sugar and potassium chlorate, producing a flame to ignite the fuse and percussion cap. Set the mine in a road with a board attached to the plunger. The first vehicle or pedestrian to pass over ignites the charge.

32. *How do you make a time bomb?*
— Use the same system as for the land mine, adapting to the fuse a connection to drive the plunger with an alarm clock, whose alarm bell of course will be removed.

33. *How do you make a delayed action fire bomb?*
— Take a small bottle and fill it with sulfuric acid; then cap it with a wad of cloth or newspaper (one page). The paper is attached to the bottle with a rubber band. Cut off the end of the cover that sticks out. This is done so that the acid is not wasted in this material. Then take another small bottle with a slightly larger mouth so that the top of the first bottle can fit into it. Into the second bottle put twelve tablespoons of potassium chlorate and four of ordinary sugar. Mix up the sugar and potassium chlorate. Now set the first bottle upside down in the mouth of the second. The acid eats through the paper or cloth and on reaching the potassium chlorate and sugar, produces a large multicolored and long-lasting flame. If we have taken the precaution to set the bottles next to inflammable materials, we are assured of a good blaze.

34. *What happens if acid and glycerine are used instead of acid alone?*
— The action of the bomb can be delayed up to five or six days depending upon the amount of glycerine to acid. Experiments with different mixtures should be made to establish formulae for various time durations.

35. *How can you obtain the maximum delay?*
— By putting the sulfuric acid into a covered bottle with a siphon in the top which reaches well below the level of the acid inside. The acid slowly evaporates on contact with the air and consequently fills the siphon with vapor. Later, the vapor condenses and drips onto the chlorate in an adjoining bottle, producing the combustion. A bomb like this can be set to explode weeks or months later.

36. *What is the principle of the military time fuse?*
— Military time fuses which can produce results days, weeks, or even months later are used by all modern armies. The triggering device consists of a plunger on a compressed spring. Acid eats at the wire compressing the spring. When the wire is cut through, the released spring drives the plunger into a priming tube containing the combustible acid, touching off the bomb. This was the type bomb used by the anti-Nazis against Hitler in 1943. The attempt to blow up the German dictator's plane failed due to the discovery of the bomb by vigilant crew members.

37. *How do you make an incendiary bomb?*
— Incendiary bombs should be used by the masses to insure our victory. Every man, woman, and child should know how to handle them. By converting everyone into a combatant and hurling thousands of incendiary bombs against the defenders of tyranny, no enemy can stand before us and victory will certainly be ours.

An incendiary bomb can be made with any kind of a bottle, a rag fuse, and gasoline. These can easily be found in any town. Fill the bottle with gasoline and put in a piece of cloth; any size will do so long as it reaches the bottom and has a bit sticking out to light. The bottle is closed with a cork stopper, paper, cloth, or can even be left open. Light the fuse and throw the bottle at the target. When it breaks open on striking the hard surface, the gas is spilled out and ignites. There is first a huge flame and small explosion which cannot hurt the thrower, even though he is close by. The flame lasts a few minutes depending upon the amount of gasoline in the bottle. The bottle with its lighted fuse, whether uncovered or not, *never explodes*. It makes no difference whether the bottle is open or covered, the gas fills a third, a half, or two-thirds of the container, or whether the bottle is carried around for hours. It will not explode in your hands.

We emphasize this so that the future bomb throwers will know that only those on the receiving end can be injured by this bomb. It is advisable to cover the bottle, however, so that upon being thrown no gasoline spills out on the ground, but all of it hits the objective. Suggested training exercises include using a bottleful of water to begin with, though actually lighting the fuse each time. Using a thick glass bottle, like the Coca-Cola ones, practice throwing as far as possible over soft earth. Plowed earth makes a good "range" to practice on. Thus you can use the same bottle many times over, practicing daily for accuracy and distance. Later, practice with different-size bottles to achieve versatility. In actual combat conditions thin-walled bottles are best as they require less energy to smash on reaching the target.

Incendiary bombs can be used to good effect at night since their flames illuminate the enemy objective and thus help make the bomb thrower's position less visible.

When attacking the military garrison in a town, the revolutionaries should proceed as follows: Everyone at a predetermined time will appear on all the surrounding flat-roofed buildings. Five minutes later everyone lets fly with a rain of incendiary bombs against all the walls of the building, trying to hit doors and windows. Revolutionaries in the streets also hurl the bombs they can against the walls at the same time, trying for the same prime targets. Especially those in the streets will throw rocks and shoot at doors, balconies, and windows.

If the police or soldiers come out they will be riddled with bullets, rocks, and bombs by the whole populaces, and especially by those on rooftops. Outnumbered like this, not one garrison can hold out.

If the garrison is constructed of wood, fire bombs can be used to good effect no matter where they hit; but even in this case doors and windows should be the prime targets. Even uncapped bottles can be used without having to light the fuses first, if a good blaze is already going. Gasoline can even be thrown in cans and earthen pots. It is well to have our revolutionaries also practice with slings, as do shepherds and country folk, so they can hurl gasoline bombs with them. You make a sling with a piece of rope two yards long, into the middle of which you attach a can, piece of heavy cloth, or leather pouch (from a handbag, etc.) where the missile is placed. We then tie one end of the rope to the right wrist. Put the gasoline bottle into the pouch (or even into a partially unwoven and widened section in the middle of the rope). Grabbing both ends of the rope, swing the sling with the bottle around your head (like hill people do all over when they want to hit a hog, bull, or horse) until you build up speed. When ready, take aim and release the free end of the rope, sending your projectile smashing into its target. That is, if you have been practicing!

Time spent in practicing bomb-throwing with a sling is really worthwhile. You can become invaluable to the revolutionary cause as a precision bomb marksman being much more valuable than the hand thrower.

Another way of throwing fire bombs is with large launchers similar to the slingshots used by children in hunting birds. The elastic bands of course must be heavier and more powerful.

Patriots in towns should become skilled in throwing fire bombs by hand, sling and slingshots; then engage in contests with one another. It goes without saying that all this is to be carried out under the utmost secrecy and with the least possible noise so as not to arouse the suspicions of the police.

These marksmen will be in the front line when the revolution comes.

When the day of the revolution comes, these units should attack the town garrison, the houses, and other places the enemy is holding out. If all the enemy strongholds in your town are immediately smashed, the whole bomb squad should report together immediately afterwards at other localities where their services are needed. If all the objectives (town garrisons, barracks, forts, etc.) are successfully taken, the Revolutionary Command will assign them to the highways to attack, from a distance, all vehicles moving through the area. These operations are best carried out in daylight and from ambush. Other bomb throwers should be ready to defend the first attackers should enemy parties pursue them from the highway.

Ideally, every revolutionary, man woman, or child (over twelve), should know how to wield incendiary bombs. To achieve this goal, not one day should go by without our practicing with water-filled bottles.

In order to prepare for the eventual battle of liberation from the forces of oppression, exploitation, and the bourgeois dictatorship, all revolutionaries should continue collecting all the empty bottles they can (even buying them), as well as storing gasoline, old rags, and matches so that when the crucial day arrives nothing will be wanting. Empty cans and cardboard boxes, well lined with paper so that no liquid comes through, should be kept. Wooden boxes can be made if bottles and pots are unavailable.

Teamwork makes for efficient fire bomb attacks. Comrades should aid the bomb thrower; some filling the containers with gasoline; others sticking in fuses; others closing the bottles with corks, paper, or rags; and still others lighting the fuses.

In a fire bomb attack, our people should be well hidden so that the police or soldiers, when driven from their refuges by the heat and flames, can be fired upon with rifles, pistols, and rocks and given the warm reception they deserve.

If, after the bombardment, there still remain inside the garrison enemies who have not surrendered, then platoons of volunteer machete men should rush in, being careful to divide up the rooms to be attacked. Some will only go down the main corridors, others into the rooms on the left, others into the ones on the right. As soon as they have eliminated the enemy occupants of the rooms, they should cut a hole no more than a yard from the floor to let their comrades in the next room know they are in command there and not to use fire bombs against them. When one side of a garrison is in our power, the revolutionaries should come out into the street to help the others attacking the other sides. This draws enemy fire and attention from our forces inside and thus shares the burden of the siege.

38. *How can communication be organized between various guerrilla sectors?*
— Portable walkie talkie radios are used by wireless experts these days for communication among groups in the field.

It is understandable that for guerrillas who have to scale high mountains and engage in long marches heavy communication equipment is out! We cannot count on vehicles to carry the equipment, nor even on hand generators which are also heavy. For our operations we are limited to only the lightest of apparatus, working off dry cells. Even these need to be replaced. The 114 mc. (two-meter) band is the best. On the air, keep your messages clear and to the point to guarantee speed and security in communication.

Groups in the field should communicate with each other directly and privately. Each group should carry a small transmitter-receiver and maintain contact on a previously determined wave length adjusted on their sets by means of a crystal oscillator. Other groups intercommunicate with one another in the same way. If various groups gather in one place they can contact a shelter or supply depot over the same system to acquire more and better equipment and aid.

When making preliminary incursions in unfriendly territory it is not advisable to complicate this basic system of communications. Radio sets can be acquired or even built, and tested before their being put to use. Sets measuring 2½ x 3½ x 10 inches powered by a 3-volt A battery and a 90-volt B battery have a 15-mile range and, in favorable conditions, twice as far.

The sets are delicate, precision-made instruments, and should be handled with care.

39. *How should guerrillas report current developments to their superiors?*
— Each guerrilla leader should report such happenings on three different

sheets. One of them furnishes valuable *personnel* information; another lists the *materiel* on hand at the moment of its signature; and the third concerns *political military* information from the sector. This last report might include the latest rumors, enemy troop movements, new men who have joined us, data on informers and spies, etc. These three parts are sent to the chiefs of the personnel section, the materiel and armament section, and the intelligence section, respectively.

40. *How should guerrillas in neighboring sectors communicate with one another?*
— They should report their strength and the state of their supplies. These reports should be delivered verbally and in person by liaison officers of the utmost confidence. The officers should also have the authority from their superiors to set the day and hour for combined operations, including their own and another or possibly two other units.

41. *Should reports be made in code?*
— It is advisable to code messages which might be captured by the enemy. Usually duplicate messages are sent, cast in special language. Two men, or better yet, two boys start out at different times with the same message. These runners should be natives of the region, clever fellows and fleet of foot.

42. *What is the complement of a guerrilla company?*
— The tactical unit designated as the company contains one hundred men including the commander, a captain. A company has four lieutenants, each commanding a section. Including their lieutenants in command, the first three sections each contain twenty-five men, except for the last. The captain is the twenty-fifth member of the fourth company.

Each section has two sergeants who in turn command a platoon apiece of eleven men. Each platoon has two corporals who command squads of five men each. In the squads a second corporal assists the corporals.

43. *What is the complement of a battalion?*
— A battalion has five companies. In the fifth company are the cooks, helpers, mechanics, barbers, tailors, cobblers, office personnel, and all those who because of the nature of their work are relieved of instruction and daily activities. Of course even this company reports for duty when the guerrilla war has attained the magnitude approaching a civil war. In other respects, the fifth company is like any other.

44. *Is it necessary for all guerrilla companies to keep this same complement?*
— In order to have complete and precise control over all units it is indispensable. If all the units are the same size you can at all times know your total strength. The quartermaster, for example, must know that three companies contain exactly 300 men, etc., without having to make any calculations. All units can then contribute equally in whatever they are called on to perform. An undermanned company could not be expected to obtain the same results as one fully staffed. Also important: no guerrilla wants to be held back in his career for having been associated with an ineffectual outfit.

45. *When your complement is full and you still have extra men, what do you do with them?*
— Report the fact at once to your immediate superior so that he can order the men sent to other units as yet undermanned. If, after all units have been brought up to full strength you still have extras, then new units can be made up with the additional men.

46. *If we have said previously that the ideal guerrilla unit in the interest of mobility is composed of fifteen men, why are we now talking of companies of one hundred?*
— Because this organization has nothing to do with combat operational necessities. A captain can command a hundred men, but does not have to use all of them together. On certain occasions, for example, in the siege of an army or police garrison defended by a small detachment, it is a good idea to use the whole guerrilla company for the assault. The captain who operates in certain sectors assigned to him by the Guerrilla Staff has his platoons of twelve men trained to be perfect guerrillas; he will sometimes utilize groups of twenty-five men commanded by lieutenants.

47. *What is the best procedure for replacing battle casualties?*
— The captain should have in some strategic site, out of the enemy's range, if possible, a training base where new guerrillas spend all their time undergoing intensive training, including the memorization of this manual and other necessary information. After having tested these trainees, a ranking will be made according to each man's knowledge, aptitudes, and intelligence section report. As necessary, to fill vacancies, the new men are then sent to active units. After reporting to the captain in charge they are given their permanent assignments.

48. *What are close order and extended order drill?*
— Close order drill is a type of exercise designed to instill habits of discipline in the troops. The guerrilla must surrender his own will completely to the one in command, no matter who it may be. While close order drill is part of the training of armies all over the world, it is no longer employed in combat. It is merely a preliminary form of exercise and does produce good results. Extended order drill is used in the field to deploy troops in the various positions of combat formations.

49. *If while on the march, in camp, or at any other time you are fired upon by the enemy, what is your first move?*
— The first thing to do is to hit the ground and as best you can lie facing the direction the shots are coming from. Then space yourself as far as possible from your comrades who will be doing the same. Thus if the enemy fire misses the one aimed at, there is no possibility of a lucky hit on another man.

After this choose the best protection within reach and take cover. If you are a captain or in command of a smaller unit, order your men to take cover as well. Do not counterattack, but try to find some way out of the ambush as quickly as possible. If the fire is too heavy and the enemy is not cutting down our men, because of lack of morale, or in fear of our return fire (which will probably be the case), you might sit tight and wait for nightfall. A daylight retreat would probably cost you too many casualties. After dark, slip out of the trap.

50. *What shall we do with our dead and wounded in the field?*
— If we have time, we will bury our dead, first seeing to it that our wounded are removed from the scene of combat; and when possible, taken to where our comrades can administer medical treatment. If there is no time nor possibility for burial of the dead, we must face the necessity of leaving them. When absolutely imperative, we leave a dead companion; but never one who is wounded.

51. *What should we do so as not to lose visual contact with the enemy?*
— When you withdraw, leave one or two men (better one than two) to keep an eye on the enemy. These observers should never open fire on the enemy, but rather do nothing to let him know he is being watched. When the enemy makes camp for the night one of the observers should report the enemy position so that some of our men can be sent to harass them during the night.

52. If the enemy continues marching during the night, what should we do?
— In that case we will follow him, keeping him in sight. The party we send out to follow him should stick as close as possible to him, maintaining harassing tactics as he marches. If the enemy later makes camp or stops to rest or eat, we continue annoying him.

53. How many men should the harassing party contain?
— Very few—perhaps two or three. The rest of our men should get their sleep. Our snipers, taking care not to be surrounded, will spend the night firing into the enemy. We will cover both of our flanks while they are resting, so that the snipers can do their job without unexpected risks. This harassment should be carried out every night without fail. You would not be doing your duty if you overlook it.

54. What is the difference between a spy and a counterspy?
— Espionage and counterespionage are arts which all guerrillas should become proficient in, since wars are not won only by using one's head, but also by using one's foot in tripping up the enemy as often as possible. A spy is a peasant working for us who accompanies the enemy troop pretending to be their friends and selling them anything they need. The type of article sold or his profits or losses are of no consequence. The important thing is that he become friendly with as many of the enemy, of all ranks as possible. He should never ask them for any information whatsoever, but rather report everything, every movement, he sees; about the equipment the enemy has; information on their delays, etc. Women are invaluable in this role. That is after they have had the proper training. Their reports should be brought in by intermediaries, and in code. If the information is of extreme urgency, by oral message. A counterspy is one who works with the enemy forces, or is a volunteer in the ranks of the oppressors. Once in their confidence, he goes to work for us, keeping us up to date with firsthand intelligence information.

In wartime, counterespionage is of greater service than simple espionage.

55. How is a secret society formed?
— A secret society is always formed with a maximum of three members. A fourth member is never admitted, but one can operate with two members. Experience has shown that anything can be done with three agents; any more get in each other's way. Besides if we have the misfortune (and

it is to a certain extent inevitable) to have one of our cells infiltrated by a spy, the most that are lost to us are two agents. This does not represent too great a risk nor expense. We must abolish those cells containing eight to ten where each member is in turn the leader of another cell with ten or twelve members, and so on.

56. *How does the sabotage section operate?*
— A secret society will never be given more than one mission. Giving the cells many of them has always produced poor results. Each society should choose a special name for identification purposes, such as José Antonio Galán, Antonio Nariño, or names of other martyrs to our cause. The sabotage section will assign but one mission to each such cell. This way they will have ample opportunity to do a good job.

57. *Does only the sabotage section have secret societies?*
— No. The Intelligence Section can and should have their information-gathering suborganizations, but these never engage in sabotage.

58. *How many types of guerrillas are there?*
— Two types: Field troops and farm troops.

59. *What are farm troops?*
— Farm troops are those who work as farm hands, apparently neutrals politically, who operate periodically, perhaps two or three times a month. They get their arms from the cache, carry out a night mission, then return to the farm and go to work the next day as though nothing had happened. If questioned, they know nothing of the operation, but all say they have seen a few armed men at a distance whom they thought to be guerrillas.

60. *How can you blow up sizable buildings, barracks, etc?*
— The easiest, surest, and least dangerous way to blow up big barracks or buildings like the Presidential Palace is by digging a tunnel ending just below the center of the building.

61. *How do you dig the tunnel?*
— First one must select a house in the neighborhood. It doesn't matter if the house is not too close to the objective. It might be more dangerous if the house is not close since the larger the distance to the objective the bigger the risk, but distance might help in order to ensure the operation without arousing suspicions. Once the house is obtained the tunnel can be

started from it, but before anything else is done canned food should be acquired and kept in the house. Food should be enough for the four or five men who are to dig the tunnel, however these men should not give the impression of being the tenants of the house.

On the first day a shaft has to be made in one of the rooms of the house reaching farther down if the building to blow is very big, and less if the building is not as heavy. Introduce in the shaft a log shaped like an E without the middle line, the one in between, the log looks then like a C with the top and the bottom straightened. The top arm of the log must be oriented toward the objective and consequently the parallel bottom arm will equally point toward the objective. The tunnel must be started in this direction and only one man will work in the shaft since it has to be narrow in order to avoid earth slides. When this man has dug out enough earth, a second man will remove it with a shovel and a third man will take it out of the tunnel with a basket. This operation will go on until the tunnel has become long enough.

62. *What do you do with the earth removed?*
— When the blasting takes place within a city it is hard to take the earth out of the house without being noticed since in these cases you have to handle a great deal of earth. The best way to handle it is by simulating in the house a business that requires loading and unloading operations. This way sandbags can be taken to an unnoticeable place or preferably cast into the river, the sea, etc.

63. *How long does it take to dig a tunnel?*
— When the earth is of average hardness a man can remove a cubic meter of earth per hour. It is easy to determine how long it will take to cover the distance between the house and the objective.

64. *How do you estimate the distance to the objective?*
— An exact calculation requires a comrade with some knowledge of trigonometry and of how to resolve triangles. Otherwise you will have to use your eyes and discuss repeated measurements with other comrades until the estimate is as accurate as desired.

65. *How much dynamite has to be placed below the building to blow it out?*
It depends on how heavy the building is but it is better not to underestimate the amount. Let's say that it is safe to use 500 to 1000 kilos of dynamite.

66. *How do you go about blasting?*

— A technician should be in charge of the operation, but everybody should know that the dynamite will only blow by means of a fulminant detonator inserted into the load and in contact with a fuse that will carry the fire from afar. To ensure the blasting it is better to use two different detonators and two fuses, and if one fails use the other.

67. *How do you place the detonator in the dynamite?*

— Pick up a sharp stick and make a hole in the dynamite, then place the detonator in the hole. Don't ever use metalic tools to open the hole unless you want to go to heaven instead of fighting in the guerrilla.

68. *How do you attach the fuse to the detonator?*

— The fuse is introduced in the open side of the detonator and is fixed with special pliers (crimpers) pressing evenly around the open side of the detonator, which prevents loosening of the fuse and failure of the blasting. If pliers are not available at blasting time bite the detonator, it is not dangerous, it is the most common method among guerrilla men.

69. *What would happen if dynamite burns or is exposed to fire?*

— It doesn't blast, it is just consumed as a melting sugar lump.

70. *How do you burn the fuse?*

— With a cigarette, and if there are two fuses both must be burned simultaneously.

71. *How can you achieve a sympathetic blasting?*

— The formula for sympathetic blasting is $S = 0.9 \times K$ (Kilos). The number of kilos of the load multiplied by 0.9 will give us the distance in meters (ms) from where to blast the other bomb. If the bomb weighs 23 kilos, multiplying 23 by 0.9 the result will be 20.7. Any bomb exploding within this distance will make the other blow up, but if we increase the distance no matter how well prepared the bomb is it will not explode.

72. *What precautions must the chief of the force have in mind before the blasting is ordered?*

— He must send an officer to every tunnel to make sure that nobody is still there, he will also make sure that each man knows what to do the minute he hears the blast. He will make a speech to encourage speed in the assault and will indicate that shameful acts during the attack will be severely punished.

73. What else should be kept in mind for after the explosion?
— Before lighting the fuse the chief will announce to the troop that the blasting time has arrived and, immediately after the explosion, all our fighters will approach the building to be taken from all sides, taking advantage of the confusion that will necessarily follow the explosion. This attack must be carried out fast for better results.

74. What is to be done with used cartridges?
— We better keep them, we can always find an officer or a sergeant among the enemy who will exchange them for new ones to make friends with us. He can very well say that they were used by his own troops in order to turn them in and get a resupply; besides, we must not keep the enemy informed about the state of our supply by letting them know how many shots were made.

75. If our fighters could take advantage of a plain to build an airfield, how would they go about it?
— The terrain must be cleared of stones, holes straightened, and hills made even. The field selected must be 1000 meters long and some 400 meters wide. Close obstacles like trees, telegraph poles, etc., must be removed.

76. How can the field be made available for the use of our planes?
— First it will be convenient to send our side information about the existence of the field, and a chart of it indicating its exact dimensions and location in a chart at a scale of 1/10,000; if possible send also a photograph. When we get news of the day and hour in which our planes will land on the field, right on that day logs and branches of trees will be placed around the perimeter of the field. As the plane appears on the horizon at the fixed hour, signals will be made with a whistle or a flag and the logs set on fire so that the plane may find the field, determine its limits as pointed out by the fires and find out the direction of the wind, since landing must be made always against the wind.

As soon as the plane has landed all the fires will be put out, things transported by the plane unloaded and the plane itself pushed by hand to the extreme end of the field where it will be again facing the wind. Only then, if the pilot requests it, which he shouldn't, a single fire will be set to indicate the direction of the wind in case the pilot cannot determine it himself by using a handkerchief. The pilot will see to it that the plane does not remain longer than necessary in order to prevent identification.

If there were any mountains around the field we will place a machine gun on the top to harass enemy airplanes that might appear on the horizon.

77. What is to be done if the plane must land during the night for security reasons?
— At the day and the hour which the plane will be directly over the field we will light the fires and keep somebody minding the fires so that they are burning constantly to let the pilot know where to land. Night landing is usually very dangerous for the pilot, since even with a good compass precise positioning over the field is always hard to achieve due to the winds which might deviate the plane without allowing the pilot to find the field. To prevent this from happening, landing may be fixed at an hour that will allow the pilot some visibility. Landings will be accordingly fixed for one hour before dawn, unless repeated utilization of the field by the same pilot makes disorientation improbable, in which case landing may be fixed for an earlier time.

After a night landing, whistles or a shot will indicate that it is time to put the fires out. If it is still dark after unloading and the plane must leave, fires will be started again all along the runway for good orientation and put out when the plane has been for fifteen minutes in the air.

78. How does a plane take off and land?
— Always facing the wind.

79. How will our men be busy when there is no immediate task?
— They will relax during the day, wash their feet daily and take care of their toenails since feet and legs are the engines of the guerrilla. They will study the maps of the region, memorizing the names of all nearby villages, and their population and some of the names of the people, they will identify on a blank chart all rivers, tributary rivers, springs, reservoirs, and wells. They will learn the distances between different points within that sector and the location of bridges and sewers that might be used for train sabotage. In other words they must learn by heart whatever piece of information might be helpful to carry on the war or to facilitate the tasks of other sections of the militia.

80. How are they given such training?
— They are first enlisted as bomb and machete men and will go with us on the marches. Beginning as scouts and carriers of water and ammunition for the guerrilla, then they will take over the watching as sentinels while the fighters rest and will be given rifles for the moment in the capacity of fighters for the first time. Then they will be employed in assaults on the police headquarters or refuges of counterrevolutionary forces, etc.

Finally when new rifles captured from the enemy are available, they will be given the rifles and promoted to guerrilla fighters.

81. *What is the standard procedure to administer capital punishment to traitors?*
— They must be given an opportunity to defend themselves, and as in the army, the regular procedures of a court martial will be followed.

82. *What are we supposed to do with sick comrades?*
— When a comrade is sick we will leave him with a family that can be trusted if they make themselves responsible for his cure and protection. They will be better off hiding in some place other than peasant huts even though attended by the peasants.

83. *What is understood by the term resupply storage?*
— Weapon and ammunition officers will keep their supplies hidden in secret places or buried close to peasants' huts.
Since it is better not to keep all the eggs in the same basket lest they be broken, resupply storages will be dispersed in strategic sectors so that we may have recourse to the supplies regardless of our position at any moment.

84. *What is the attitude of the fighters with regard to peasants?*
— All food taken from them must be paid for at a good price, thanks must be repeatedly expressed and peasants made aware that they are helping their own cause. Our men will try to repair things in the house such as beds, closets, tables that might be ruined. They will help the peasant in fencing his lot or in sowing or clearing the fields, and in so doing they will clearly show our sympathy and attract the peasants to our cause so that we may eventually request their help any time.

85. *How is the defense of a town taken from the enemy organized?*
— In order to organize this defense, the town must be rearranged to take the configuration of a complex of fortifications by opening connecting passages between adjacent houses. These passages must be small, letting only one man crouching go through, so that if it is an enemy he can be easily disposed of and if it is a friend he may go through with only the relative discomfort of bending his knees. Once all the houses are connected, those facing the street where the enemy will attack first will have in the front several holes like small vents from which to shoot. These

openings will be made at a level higher than the regular stature of a man so that even bullets that occasionally go through them will not hit our men. Of course, in order to shoot from these openings one must be standing on a chair.

86. *What will be our attitude toward the population of the town?*
— We will try to convince them gently that they must evacuate their houses, that it is an imperative of the war to fortify them. If this can't be achieved peacefully then they will be evacuated by force as an imperative of war.

87. *What will be done with the furniture?*
— All the furniture, good or bad, will be used to connect houses of separate blocks. Blocks must be connected by barricades made of furniture, stones, bricks, etc.

88. *What about military defensive organization?*
— The chief of highest seniority or rank will appoint his deputies for different sectors of the captured town that is to be defended. Every chief responsible for a sector will see to it that houses and blocks are prepared to conform to the specified defense configuration.

89. *What will be the role of the groups operating in the vicinity of the town during the course of the enemy attack?*
— They will be in constant activity, striking at the rear guard of the besiegers and most of all their supply sources.

90. *How can we slow down the capture of entire blocks by the enemy?*
— We will have parapets in the corners of all the roofs and firing from them will deny the enemy access to the houses. We will also have in the houses dry husk and rags impregnated with cheap oil. If a house is taken, the husk set on fire will have the effect of a smoke grenade stopping enemy advance.

91. *How long can we keep defending a town in this manner?*
— It may last for years. This was the type of defense put into practice during the defense of the University district of Madrid; Franco's troops never went through it.

92. *What if the enemy completely cuts the water supply to the town?*
— It was presupposed that the activity of the outside guerrillas would

make it frightful and unacceptable for the enemy to maintain a protracted assault; however, if after all there is no other alternative the best way to escape is to break through the enemy lines in the middle of the dark and flee to the hills.

93. *Which must be the main concern of the fighter while in the hills?*
— His main concern must be the care of his gun, since the weapon is his friend and protector, his means of survival. The rifle must be kept clean and oiled, especially when you are out in the country, marching by dusty paths where guns easily get dirty.

94. *Who can be properly called a hill fighter?*
— He who is in open and declared rebellion against the oligarchy, against bourgeois dictatorship, against the people's enemies; in other words, all regular soldiers in the guerrilla who wage war against oppression and exploitation.

95. *Which is the maximum time for a guerrilla to remain in the same place?*
— Three days is the longest they can stay in one particular place. On the third day they must start toward a position far away from their previous one.

96. *What qualifications make a perfect guerrilla fighter?*
— To correctly handle a gun, a rifle, a machine gun, and a revolver.
   To be able to fight with a knife and fence with a stick.
   To be able to throw a knife well and hit a distant target.
   Horseback riding, bicycle driving, automobile driving.
   Making and using bombs.
   Know how to take and develop pictures.
   Know how to use the phone.
   Typing.
   Chart designing.
   An elementary knowledge of topography.
   Know how to read a chart and interpret contour data.
   Know how to whistle loudly.
   Practice in climbing ramparts and walls using ropes or human towers.
   Practice in twelve-hour marches through rugged hills with slight descents.
   Swimming, rowing, motor boat driving.
   Practice in climbing trees and telegraph poles rapidly.

Familiarization with piston-engine parts.

Know how to start a car with a crank, how to reach the fuel tank, how to fill the tires of a car or a bicycle, how to change the tires fast.

Know the Morse Code.

Know how to start the propeller of a light plane.

Extreme tolerance to all religions.

Finally to be courageous, daring, cunning, to anticipate needs and dangers, to avoid ties with things or persons; to love danger.

97. *Are all those conditions indispensable to become a guerrilla fighter?*
— Those are qualities of the perfect fighter only and are only achieved at the peak of the fighter's performance. Take Pancho Villa for instance. He was an outstanding fighter and nevertheless he was an illiterate. However, all those qualifications must be required as an ideal, as they are required by military academies to graduate officers who can defend the fatherland in case of aggression.

98. *What items should be on hand for the guerrilla?*
— The perfect guerrilla must have:

Combat boots for the men.

Thick socks.

Pants reenforced with inside and back patches.

Thick and resistant belts that eventually can be joined together as the links of a chain and be used in crossing rivers, climbing walls and obstacles . . . They are called "tails" by the fighters.

Coats according to the weather (jackets).

Compasses.

Good watches.

Knives and folding knives.

Scissors to cut hair.

Scissors to cut nails (especially toenails).

Soap for clothes washing.

Guns, submachine guns.

Grenades.

Combat binoculars.

Medicaments proper for the guerrilla in the first aid kit.

Pliers with oilskin handle (you can also use a thin pipe to cover the handle).

Hatchets to cut wood.

Razors and blades.

Flashlights.

Forehead lights (of the kind that can be attached to the head, as the
   miners do).
Batteries for all these lights.
Three-corner files.
Saws.
Threads and fishhooks for fishing.
Lighters.
Hammocks.
Wirecutters.

99. *Isn't that too much to be carried by the fighters?*
— For sure, but it can be taken by the irregulars who always accompany
the guerrilla. The list is just a catalog of things that we should have on
hand at one time or another and that eventually will all be needed, but
that doesn't necessarily mean that all of them should be taken in every raid.

100. *What precautions must we have before attacking a village?*
— In order to attack a village we must know first all the details about it.
Some of the most important details will be:
   Whether or not it has telegraph or telephone communications. Whether
      or not there are troops guarding communication centers.
   If there are no troops to guard them, where (how far) is the closest
      communication center.
   How many civilians have rifles.
   Whether there is in the village an amateur radio transmitter.
   Names of traitors and executioners, domiciles of the best known op-
      pressors of patriotic and revolutionary agents.
   Location of the railway or road bridges closest to the village and size
      of the guard.
   Distance to the closest airfield.
   Timetable of trains passing through the village and of trucks or buses
      of lines regularly serving the town.
   Analysis of the topography of the local area and all other useful data
      that could possibly be collected.
Once the information has been gathered, the data should go into the
Staff Section (Operations), which will prepare plans for the assault based
on the information received. Assaults are possible without all these re-
quirements, but this is the technical approach that will give us the highest
probability of success.

101. *Once plans have been prepared how does the operation develop?*
— The precise time must be fixed. Each special task is assigned to a special

team. These teams must operate fast and with decision, without being concerned with the development of the operations of the other teams, or with the failure of these operations. A team will cut telegraph and telephone communications at the entrance of the village, another team will cut them at the exit. Since individuals possessing weapons are known, a team guided by friendly villagers will break into the houses of these individuals and take their weapons along. The addresses of these individuals and the order in which these searches will take place will be specified in the lists that the chief of the team will be given. Other teams will pick up squealers, spies, or traitors.

All these things must be done "electrically," that is, in the least possible time, and the faster we do it the greater the success will be, even in terms of convincing the enemy about our great discipline and morals. This way hopeful revolutionaries will see with their own eyes that our organization can do the job. After the operation is finished we will leave the village by car, meeting the vehicles in predetermined places where they will be waiting with their engines running.

102. *What will be the mission of a guerrilla chief in an area under control?*
— He will organize, under the guidance of the recruiting officer, several groups with the following purposes:
A. One unit will "comb" the area, that is, it will inspect all the houses and sectors where there are enemies of the people's cause. This same unit will carry out the requisition of all the combat elements that we may need by searching wherever they may be.
B. Another unit will intensify propaganda for our cause in that area. Both units will be integrated by honest personnel who are notoriously incapable of stealing or of abusing those whom they dislike or their personal enemies.

103. *What will be the punishment for those who commit abuses?*
— Those who would dare to steal in these circumstances, or perpetrate abuses or infractions, must immediately undergo a drum-head court martial and after conviction sent to the firing squad without wasting any time.

104. *How will the execution take place?*
— It will take place at an hour that will permit attendance of a large audience. It will be publicly announced and dramatically set. An officer will address the crowd explaining that the man to be shot is guilty of rape, murder, theft, or of any other shameful and antirevolutionary action that

he may have accomplished. He will use this occasion to emphasize the honesty of the People's Army and praise it in the most laudatory terms insisting upon the fact that shameful acts against the dignity of the people will never be left without their rigorous and well deserved punishment.

105. *What is the most important advice that should never be overlooked in the marches?*
— Combat marches will mainly be accomplished during the night, especially when our purpose is to be seen again far away from our previous position and let the enemy think that there are two different units in operation. During the day we will be sleeping, studying, or occupied in activities proper of the guerrilla, such as care of the weapons, distribution of ammunition, care of the feet, study of the map of the region, attention to the business of the sections of the guerrilla, memorizing names of nearby villages or individuals living within the sector, etc. Don't forget the names of the ranches that we visit, etc. But in marching during the night it is a must that we walk in the most absolute silence and without smoking; otherwise, the entire unit might be destroyed.

106. *How must we proceed in a surprise enemy attack after taking shelter?*
— First we will try not to answer enemy fire, and then, even if they seem to be fewer than we are, wait until the day is over to retreat. If we were superior in number, we engage them for a short time and cause them some casualties. If the situation is not clear it is better to disappear because it might be a decoy or a stratagem to surround us with superior forces.

The course of action must be resolved by the chief of the guerrilla who knows by heart that our tactic is not to engage the enemy but to hit and run.

107. *Is the purpose of such skirmishes to cause casualties or to cause psychological effects?*
— Our aim is to destroy enemy morale, keeping their mercenaries from relaxing. If a troop does not sleep during the night they are worthless during the day and slow in the marches. Therefore, the enemy will not be left in peace for a single night.

108. *Shall we take turns in this mission?*
— Of course. This is a mission that should be shared by all members of the guerrilla for several reasons:
They must all share the honor of harassing the enemy, our fighters

must acquire more experience in this type of actions to improve their morale, and finally it is known that when a soldier does not shoot he gets more and more paralyzed, rusty, useless.

109. *Which is the most vulnerable part of a camp?*
— Kitchens, stables, dispensary, etc. These are points that can't be defended and where the combat morale would be lower.

110. *How will we keep weapons in a peasant hut?*
— It would be a big mistake to keep it in boxes in the hut itself. They must be buried in boxes with an inner cover of zinc, in other words the box will be patched up inside with straightened oil or gasoline cans that will be nailed to the box. The weapons should be wrapped in rags if time permits. Then the box must be closed tight and well hidden in the hole. There you have your hideaway.

111. *How deep should the boxes be buried?*
— Always rather deep to prevent any soldiers from digging around the field close to the house and finding the boxes there (although even this is improbable).

112. *How far from the house should the boxes be buried?*
— Rather far, between 30 and 60 meters from the house, and the place will be known only by the man who buried them and two other fighters; one of whom must always be from the weapons section and the other will, in each case, be from a different one.

113. *What should be done from time to time in order to prevent rifles from getting rusty when in use?*
— They should be examined by the weapons expert that always goes along with the guerrilla and in all cases the fighter must take care of his own weapon with love and dedication, for it is an insurance policy for his life and for those who are in his company.

114. *How many times a week do the chiefs of the sections report to the commander of the guerrilla?*
— Twice a week, during the stops in the marches, the commander will call his chiefs of sections away from the rest of the comrades in a spot called the "office," close to a rock or a tree; the commander will talk with each one of his chiefs separately, starting with the Information chief. The commander will ask as many questions as he thinks fit. One after the other

all the chiefs will be examined by the commander about the status of every branch in his section and about the efficiency of their activities.

115. *What basic knowledge should the guerrilla fighter possess?*
— They all should have an idea of plotting, plot reading, contour interpretation and be able to reproduce at a different scale a map of installations or facilities such as schools, court buildings, police stations, barracks, etc.

116. *If we have on hand a map of Colombia, for instance, and we want to change it from a scale of 1:300,000 to a scale of 1:5000, what is the best way to do it?*
— Since the quotient of 300,000 divided by 5,000 is 60 it would be very hard and bothersome to enlarge the map on a paper 60 times larger than the original, and besides, many parts of the map would not be of interest for guerrilla operations. Therefore, it is better to design first a map four times larger covering only the part in which we are interested. The new scale would be 1:75,000 (300,000 divided by 4). After this we place within a square the zone of operations and enlarge it to 1:15,000; finally by a similar operation we enlarge only a concrete part of the zone of operations making it three times larger or to a scale 1:5,000. Instead of a direct 60 times enlargement, we enlarged a part of the original 4 times, a part of that 5 times and then a portion of the latter 3 times. The scale is: $4 \times 5 \times 3 = 60$ times larger.

117. *What shall we do with the maps 1:75,000 and 1:15,000 that were made and will not be used?*
— Give them to the Operations Section which can certainly use them.

118. *What does the fraction 1:100,000 mean in a map scale?*
— It means that every meter on the map will represent 100 kilometers in reality, that is, 100,000 meters on the ground.

119. *What is the best scale for maps used in guerrilla operations?*
— The best scale is 1:10,000 or 1:5,000.

120. *What acts of sabotage can be accomplished by isolated patriots?*
— Those who don't feel that they have the courage to get together and form secret societies and those who don't trust anybody around but still would like to cooperate by means of individual action may carry out the following tasks:

a. If they are working at a post office they could slow down service or send official communiques to the wrong place or in the wrong direction, always avoiding the possibility of being suspected.

b. If they work on a phone board they can boycott the service and slow it down.

c. Mailmen may pick out letters addressed to important personalities in the regime and open them by steam, learning about their contents. If they contain intelligence data they will pass these data to the Intelligence Service.

d. Phone operators will try not to miss a word of interesting conversations and will communicate all useful information to our movement. The operator should do this by telephone without disclosing her name.

e. Those who work in garages will put emery powder in the oil of automobiles used by mercenaries or by officials who are against the people. If emery were not available they may use sand or pulverized rocks, etc.

f. If they work in garages belonging to the armed forces or in official maintenance depots, they will ruin the supplies, hide the tools, misuse gas either in engine tests or by washing their hands often, always trying to throw away some.

g. If they are government chauffeurs they will try to ruin the tires with nails if they can do it in the garage or by driving close to the sidewalk to scratch their sides or by driving over rocks.

h. Schoolteachers will talk to their pupils about the greatness of progress, of beautiful ideals, about love among human beings and solidarity among nations, looking after each other even within the moral slavery in which they find themselves.

i. Everybody will pass on gossip about the exploitation that the people suffer, the increasing prices of essential goods, and complain about the miserable life they are leading.

j. Workers will ask for leave affecting sickness, and request increases in salaries or try to manufacture defective articles especially if the factories are managed by a few enemies of the working class.

k. Wherever there are no water or light meters people will leave faucets open and the lights on.

l. Government employees will not brief or correct their subordinates, instead they will criticize all orders from above and emphasize the defects of their superiors. They will use their time as much as possible in telephone conversations, coffee breaks, reading newspapers, will change the sense of documents, cause disorder, break the furniture, break machines, etc.

m. When opportune, they will change personnel, reprimand those who are friendly with the regime, and at the same time they will appear to be the most fanatic supporters of the government and of the people's enemies. They will ruin the urinaries, bathrooms, water, light, and gas installations, not only in the public offices but in cafes, casinos, theaters, etc. The best way to destroy a urinary is by throwing cotton packages and newspapers mixed with nails and wire into it.

n. In larger offices they will let loose rats and feed them with cheese until they adapt to the place and can operate by themselves. They will also try to blow the light bulbs in the offices and try to cause a short-circuit.

o. While traveling on the train or other public means of transportation they will cut the seats with razors or scissors, etc. In the stadiums or other games they will protest and disturb the peace by yelling against the authorities, the police, etc.

p. In the streets they will try to stop the traffic by going against the traffic regulations.

q. On the anniversaries of traditional commemorations that are not celebrated by the bourgeois government they will be in the streets marching past military, government, and police offices, in a silent protest against the arbitrary government of the oligarchy. They must also go to the plazas where there are statues of freedom heroes and circle around until their presence is noticed, and attract other demonstrators provoking police intervention. Then they will all start booing the police, manifesting indignation. They will convene crowds large enough to break police ranks and to expand and shrink like an accordion, rushing like gigantic waves toward the enemy only to disperse in the collision and to reorganize, forming other waves to clash with police trucks or armored cars or army tanks or "steel helmets." If there is opportunity and impunity they must boo the most prominent figures of the bourgeois landowners and the dictatorship, yelling "down with them," and encouraging revolt so as to form a massive clamor, howling and wild. The idea is to cause methodically the greatest disorder possible. If political debates with mercenaries take place try to keep the opponent surrounded by comrades, especially if he is a police official, and try to out-yell him and out-act him.

121. *What is to be done if the police or the troops open fire on the people?*
— If in a street fight either the police, the armed forces, or the "steel helmets" open fire against the crowd, the next day all our friends and comrades in the work must be induced not to go to work so that a protest may be transformed into a revolutionary general strike. If this end is achieved all efforts will be directed toward generalization of the strike so that bus-

iness will stop and nobody will dare to work in the factories. To this end we must recruit the help of all our friends and use coercion and energetic measures upon shy and cowardly people.

122. *How do we use rumors?*
— We echo all sorts of rumors and fibs to discredit the most prominent figures of the oligarchy, including presidents elected in a referendum, and we "improve" these rumors. They may also discredit chiefs of police, army, or secret police.

123. *How should we react in the event of a vehicle collision?*
— When we are present at the scene of a collision and one of the drivers is a government driver we must direct the indignation of the people against him.

124. *What shall we do if a fire starts?*
— If a fire starts we will attempt to interfere with the work of the firemen. We will make a call from a distant place from which escape is easy and give the firemen a wrong address. (This refers to fires due to sabotage of government facilities or of offices of prominent figures in the regime.)

125. *How can we use vacant apartments?*
— If we can get vacant apartments for rent belonging to persons in favor of the regime we will throw gasoline, or any other inflammable on hand, into them and set them on fire, escaping only after the fire starts.

126. *How do you spoil gasoline?*
— To sabotage gasoline it is sufficient to put some water or sugar in it.

127. *How do we sabotage a machine or a car?*
— To sabotage a car it is enough to take a small part essential to make it run; it is better to pick out parts that cannot be easily found in the store and must be ordered. Summing up, all efforts must be directed to paralyze regular work, whether in government offices or in private factories, especially wherever it may affect influential figures. We must never give a peaceful moment to the representatives of the criminal bourgeois dictatorship. We will never stop until we see the ultrareactionary dictatorship collapse violently and lose the power that it held for so long at the expense of the people, while the peasant and working majorities and the middle classes suffered misery and hunger and strains and worries.

128. *How do we distribute the troops in order to defend a village?*
— The village itself must be divided into four zones, each one under a responsible chief who will operate independently from the other but keeping them posted as to the steps that he takes so that they can all depend on each other although they are all subordinate to the commander of the village.

129. *How will the troop itself be divided by its commander?*
— The troop will be classified in three categories: roof shooters, balcony shooters, and window shooters.

130. *How will the sentries on the roofs react in case of an air attack?*
— They will get out of reach of the planes' machine guns, but if a plane is flying low they will open fire against it trying to be always under the cover of walls or old ramparts and aiming at the bushing of the propeller.

131. *How do we keep the doors of the houses?*
— The front doors will be all locked and if possible blocked so that the only way to get in the house is by destroying them.

132. *Should we remove all doors within the house?*
— All the doors within the house must be removed or pulled away except those of the rooms where food and ammunition are kept.

133. *How do we arrange the houses that make one block?*
— They must all be connected by passages made in the separation walls; these passages should not be higher than one meter or wider than sixty centimeters so that people can go through one by one only and stooping. This prevents the enemy from entering a house ready to attack the defenders.

134. *What shall we do about women and children living in these houses?*
— Women, children, and elderly people will be evacuated. Some women, useful old men, and children over sixteen will be allowed to stay if they want to fight for the revolutionary cause. These women and old men will be used in the many jobs and arrangements that defense requires, such as preparation of the blocks, recruiting, encouraging those who don't dare to fight, and especially distributing the ammunition, because at fighting time all men should be shooting and it should be these women who take care of providing men with ammunition.

135. *What will people evacuated from the houses be allowed to take with them?*
— All their private things, except weapons, ammunition, even if it is only shot cartridges, knives, hatchets, picks, bottles, gasoline, alcohol, or anything that might be helpful in the battle.

136. *What shall we do with requisitioned food and ammunition?*
— They will be kept in a room of the house especially adapted for this purpose, the food in one room and the ammunition in another together with everything useful in battle. Those who guard the food will be made aware that they will be responsible for every crust of bread, and will not take anything for themselves unless they want to be accused of disobedience, irresponsibilty, cheating their comrades, and of faults against the ethics of revolutionary war.

137. *Who will guard the rooms where food and ammunition are kept?*
— Both rooms will preferably be guarded by women who can be trusted with this task, since men will be dedicated to missions requiring more strength or to missions of more responsibility and risk.

138. *What kinds of communications will be maintained?*
— Communications from house to house and between the zones and the headquarters of the defense. Communications may be verbal, but it is better if it is done by writing. Other communications will be conducted by means of flags or other signals previously agreed upon, such as cloth hanging from the balconies, etc. We will also have to manage to establish communications with the guerrillas in the hills.

139. *What kind of discipline will be maintained in the confusion originated by our occupation of private quarters?*
— We will be more severe with our own men than with the population. We will shoot right away those who trespass or steal for their own pocket, and severely punish those who beat, insult, or humiliate civilians who refuse to give up their houses or goods or who don't understand our explanations for breaking into their houses. Our troops will take whatever is necessary without cruelty or insults and will evacuate people from their homes only as a necessary imposition due to the war.

140. *How do we attend to the care of the wounded?*
— The wounded from all houses will be gathered in a house well adapted

to their care that will be as far as possible from enemy fire. Since all the houses will be connected, as we said before, it will be possible to transfer the wounded from house to house and from block to block to the point where they will be attended.

141. *What shall we do if the enemy takes one house in the village?*
— We will defend the next house room by room.

142. *What if they take several blocks?*
— We will defend the village block by block until there is none left. It should be clear that this is only done in the phase of open war with the enemy and not in the phase of guerrilla warfare in which this type of combat is never admissible.

143. *What is our answer to those who argue against this phase of combat saying that we are destroying the fatherland?*
— We will contend that the best way to destroy the country is by allowing the enemies of the people from all the parties of the oligarchy to eat it up and give it up to Yankee imperialism. We will tell them that the shame of living under oppression, under the dictatorship of the bourgeoisie, is worse than to fight for the fatherland and for true freedom, even if we have to start reconstruction from scratch. Finally we will tell them that we prefer to build the new walls at the expense of the blood of our brothers rather than leave the old walls to serve as prisons for the eternal seclusion of the workers, the peasants, the students, the employees, etc.

144. *Is it convenient to have in our cause people working in counterespionage?*
— Undoubtedly. Persons in the villages who do this job will render a better service than anybody who would give us fifty machine guns.

145. *Should the counterspy take part in the battles against our own men?*
— A counterspy should take part in such battles, but his role should be to show off as much as possible without causing great damage to the guerrilla, without really hurting anybody.

146. *What services can be rendered by a counterspy who serves as an officer in the enemy ranks?*
— He may give us details about the strength of each one of the units that

follow us, names of their officers, material at their disposal, maps of the places where they are assigned, information about the morale of these troops, ammunition supply, and movements planned, etc. etc. One of the best services that he may render is to assign pickets to engage a guerrilla in places previously agreed upon among us or to leave a small garrison in a particular place, impeding their defense by leaving them short of ammunition or by leaving in command a cowardly sergeant or corporal who would waste the ammunition, or by moving their soldiers some place so that we may attack them in this way at a determined place and time, etc. An officer of the enemy forces that collaborates with us is more useful than ten of our own officers fighting the enemy. For this reason those who work in counterespionage must always volunteer to participate in actions against us or in outfits set for repression of guerrillas, such as the so-called "peace guerrillas" organized by the dictators Laureano Gómez and Rojas Pinilla, among others, in Colombia, etc.

In the Occupied Zones

147. *What precautionary steps must we take after occupation of enemy territory?*
— Small units will be formed with men that don't move as fast as the other fighters because of injuries, wounds, physical defects, or exhaustion. These units will "comb" the area. In these circumstances all the sections will be able to work efficiently, without rush or fears.

The Information Section will gather information as necessary, Operations will interrogate the peasantry about bridges and sewers and will mark them in their maps, Sabotage will increase its manpower with as many men as they please, instructing and training the men to form new secret societies. Recruitment will take care of the necessary propaganda to add new men to the guerrilla, checking with Information before making the selection. Training will carry out its mission by establishing camps, selecting and stimulating the instructors who will produce good hill fighters and refined technicians in the specialty of demolition, etc. Armament will make an inventory of the material at the disposal of the different sections, requesting and accepting from the General Staff orders to the effect that all units report to our rearguard facilities for armament inspection and repairs. Ammunition will be able to select good places for their secret storages and make a status report on their supply and will also from time to time dig out their stocks and expose them to the sun. Supply can take care of the purchases of food and will catalogue requisitioned items in their storages. All of which will be done more accurately now that the pressure of the fight is overcome. Finally, Health and Propaganda will carry out their own missions.

In Victory

148. *What will be done by the chief when he sees that victory is coming?*
— He will carefully attempt to separate those who will volunteer to fight at the last moment from those who are truly our own men. He will attempt to keep a good record of his own men and of those who in the last minute jumped onto the bandwagon of revolution. These new volunteers will be registered in a card with complete information and two pictures, and will be requested to sign their service record which will be passed to purging committees for verification.

149. *What will be the attitude of the chief toward the indignation of the masses and their intentions of revenge against the agents and spies of the people's enemies and the mercenaries of the dictatorship?*
— He will strongly and effectively oppose those attitudes, because it is prescribed that all persons suspected of being war criminals will have the right of self defense, and especially because there were many among the enemy who were secretly doing counterespionage, and risked their lives for the victory of our cause.

150. *What is the greatest danger that we face after victory over the bourgeois dictatorship and over the oppression and exploitation of the various oligarchical regimes?*
— The greatest danger is dissipation of our victory. The forces of evil and oppression, the historical legions of the reactionary classes never give up. They are like snakes that always fight back even after we step on their poisonous throats; they crawl and crouch, only to get ready to jump over the people. They never give up, they always resist, they are always trying to stifle us.

Some of these snakes are the politicians in the clergy who hardly deserve the name of Christian or Catholic. They are the ones who want to do in Latin America as they did in Spain where they achieved complete domination of the Spanish people after a horrible mass murder. And thus they preach in the Dominican Republic the slogan of God and Trujillo and have the shamelessness of repeating in our countries, exhausted by ex-

ploitation, misery, oppression, injustice, and by bourgeois reactionary
dictatorships that call themselves democratic, that heaven is for the poor
in spirit.

This clergy, by nature reactionary and always meddling in politics,
should not call itself Christian or Catholic since their only ambition is to
use religion as a cover to justify the oppression of the minorities and to
deceive the peasants and workers by forming the so-called "Christian"
and "Christian Democratic" or "Social Christian" parties, or others with
equal pretensions, and to them they preach that there should not be hatred
nor aversions, that God will judge humanity, that the conquerors should
be lenient with the defeated. It must be noted well that these individuals,
who don't believe in God or in anything of the kind, mean "the God
Capitalism," "the God Exploitation" when they mention God.

They never preach these things when it is the enemy who have their
feet on our neck, but no sooner is the war over when they will tell you
this and more. They will go around shrieking to stop our fight against
reaction if it ever makes a show; and so they will carry out their "missions" for the benefit of the enslavers. But you, revolutionary son of the
people, beware of "the incense of the sacristy."

*Watch over and mind your own victory, never let clerical winds im-
press or hypnotize you, beware of those who in all nations dominated by
capitalism or imperialism adulate and support exploiters and oppressors:
beware lest those hypocrites of the "kyrieleison" undermine your heroic
and well-deserved victory.*

[Translators' Note: Inconsistencies in the original have been translated without comment or correction.]

NOTES

Notes to the Introduction

1. A shorter version of this Introduction was published as an article by the author in the *Air University Review*.
2. Secretary of State John Hay on 22 June 1904 sent the following telegram to Samuel Gummere, American consul general in Tangier: "We want Perdicaris alive or Raisuli dead. Further than this we desire least possible complications with Morocco or other powers. You will not arrange for landing marines or seizing custom house without specific directions from this Department." Text obtained through the cooperation of Edwin S. Costrell, chief of the Historical Studies Division of the State Department's Historical Office.
3. Perhaps the first instances of hostage-taking in what was to become Latin America was the practice of the Incas of removing to their "Holy City" the images of the gods of peoples they had conquered. "Here they remained as hostages, in some sort, for the conquered nation, which would be the less inclined to forsake its allegiance, when by doing so it must leave its own gods in the hands of its enemies" (William H. Prescott, *History of the Conquest of Mexico and History of the Conquest of Peru* [New York: The Modern Library]).
4. American agricultural expert Claude L. Fly was held captive in Uruguay for a record period of nearly seven months. The "record" was broken in 1971, when British Ambassador Geoffrey Jackson was held by the Tupamaros from 8 January to 9 September.
5. General Vo Nguyen Giap, *The South Vietnam People Will Win* (Hanoi, 1965).
6. George Modelski, "Viet Minh," in C. E. Black and T. P. Thornton eds., *Communism and Revolution* (Princeton, 1964).
7. United States Mission in Viet Nam, *A Study—Viet Cong Use of Terror* (Saigon, 1967).
8. Statistical information provided by Stuart Halpine, information officer, Civil Operations and Rural Development Support, U.S. Military Assistance Command, Vietnam.
9. Douglas Pike, *The Viet-Cong Strategy of Terror* (Saigon, 1970).
10. Ibid.

11. "The Communist Manifesto" in Arthur P. Mendel, ed., *Essential Works of Marxism* (New York, 1965).
12. Karl Marx, *Capital* (International Publishers Co. edition, New York, 1967).
13. Jay Mallin, ed., *"Che" Guevara on Revolution* (Miami, 1969).
14. *Selected Military Writings of Mao Tse-tung* (Peking, 1963).
15. V. I. Lenin, "Partisan Warfare," *Orbis* (summer 1958).
16. Leon Trotsky, *Stalin* (New York, 1941).
17. "Snipers in Ambush: Police Under the Gun," *Time*, 14 September 1970.
18. "Jefferson—The Faith in Majority Rule" in Terry Hoy, ed., *Politics and Power—Who Should Rule* (New York, 1968).

Notes to *Partisan Warfare*

1. William J. Miller, Henry L. Roberts, Marshall D. Shulman, *The Meaning of Communism* (Morristown, N.J., 1963).
2. Leon Trotsky, *Stalin* (New York, 1941).
3. Ibid.

The following footnotes, prepared by Stefan T. Possony, were appended to the translated version published by *Orbis*:

1. The term "partisan war" or "partisan actions" is a euphemism. It does not mean "guerrilla war" in the modern sense but stands for terrorism, holdups and robberies. So-called "expropriations" of money were directed against banks, taxation agencies, post offices, customs houses, railroad stations and similar establishments where large sums of cash were likely to be stored. However, small firms, such as bakeries and village shops, as well as affluent individuals, also were victimized. In many instances, the "expropriations" were planned by professional "fingermen" and executed by expert robbers. Terror was practiced on policemen, soldiers and officials, both in cities and in the rural areas. Operations in the cities were conducted by small "combat groups"; forays in the countryside were sometimes executed by large armed bands which, under the convenient guise of "partisan warfare," made looting and pillaging a profitable profession. Originally, the social democrats had rejected terrorism, which was a major *modus operandi* of the social revolutionaries. During 1905 and 1906, however, the incidence of terror increased greatly and the bolshevik faction of the Social Democratic Party supported it wholeheartedly. In fact, a large percentage of the bombs used in "partisan warfare" was fabricated in a secret bolshevik laboratory run by Leonid B. Krassin. Most mensheviks were opposed both to terror and "expropriations," but it is interesting that G. V. Plekhanov, the founder of Russian Marxism, favored them, at least for a time. The Russian socialists who opposed terrorism argued that "European means of struggle" be used. They feared that terrorism was harming the reputation of the social democrats and worried about the fact that many, if not most, of the "expropriations" were perpe-

trated by criminal elements, for purposes of their own personal enrichment.

In reading Lenin's discourse, it should be remembered that, in practical terms, he was advocating an alliance between revolution and crime: Lenin did, in fact, enter into agreements with criminal elements during the partisan warfare period. Later, during World War I, he even recommended a notorious highwayman to the Germans for sabotage operations. (The man received pay but did not commit any acts of sabotage.)

While Lenin was penning his treatise on "partisan war," the terrorist phase of the first Russian revolution was reaching its peak. In October 1906 alone, 121 terror acts, 47 clashes between revolutionaries and the police, and 362 expropriations were reported. (See Boris Souvarine, *Staline, Aperçu Historique du Bolchevisme* [Paris: Plon, 1935], p. 92.) While it is impossible to draw up exact statistics of the total terror campaign, there is no question that it cost the lives of more than 5,000 policemen and officials. Several millions of rubles were "expropriated" by criminal and revolutional elements.

2. The terms, "types" or "forms of struggle," and their variations, such as "combat tactics" and "methods of battle," all of which sound awkward in English, denote a key concept in communist conflict doctrine. The term "struggle" is a short notation for "class struggle." Lenin contends that the tactics and techniques of the class struggle must be altered as situations and conditions change. Socialists should have no dogmatic attachment to one particular type of tactic or a particular weapon but should employ those procedures and means which, singly or in combination, are expedient and effective. The point is important since American policy-makers often assume that the communists are wedded to one particular "type of struggle" and that the communists, once they begin to apply one specific method, will continue to do so. Such an interpretation of bolshevik theory can be reconciled neither with the writings nor the actions of international communism.

3. Lenin alludes here to one of Friedrich Engels' last publications in which, to the chagrin of the radicals, he discussed the difficulties of an armed uprising against a government armed with modern weapons. Engels went so far as to question the usefulness of that revolutionary symbol, the barricade. Lenin also alludes to the gradual shift which at that time was taking place in practically all European socialist parties toward forsaking revolution in favor of evolutionary methods.

4. This refers to a weekly magazine entitled *Bes Zaglavia* (*Without Title*), of which sixteen issues were published between February and May 1906 by S. N. Prokopovich, E. D. Kuskova, and others. The editors of this magazine were moderate socialists who believed in democracy. They were friendly to the objectives of the left wing of the Constitutional Democrats (Cadets).

5. Lenin refers to the mass strike movement which began in August 1905 and in October culminated in one of the most complete general strikes of history. It was this strike movement, and particularly the railroad strike, which forced the Russian government to proclaim the so-called "Octo-

ber Manifesto" by which a semiconstitutional regime (Max Weber described it as "sham constitutionalism") was promulgated. Incidentally, these strikes neither were called nor run by the socialist leaders but by the liberal-bourgeois parties, especially the Cadets. Lenin's wording suggests that he was completely aware of this historical fact which, however, he was loath to admit in writing. Lenin and other revolutionaries did not return to Russia until an amnesty, late in October 1905, made it safe for them to do so. Only after the middle-of-the-road parties, whose outstanding demands were met by the "October Manifesto," withdrew from the revolution, did the socialists assume leadership of the revolutionary movement.

6. Alexander Helphand, better known as "Parvus," discussed this vexing problem of barricades as early as 1897—that is, two years after Engels had expressed his doubts. "Parvus" pointed out that barricades, while perhaps no longer militarily useful, could serve as rallying points for the aroused and fighting masses. He considered barricades as a predominantly psychological device suitable for bringing the masses into the streets. Obviously, Lenin, who feared "Parvus" as an intellectually superior competitor, did not want to give him credit for this correct prediction, nor did he want to acknowledge that he now adopted "Parvus'" interpretation of barricade tactics.

7. The "affair of 22 January 1905" is better known as "Bloody Sunday." Lenin's undramatic description of this event, which was the tragic overture to the revolution of 1905, probably is due to the fact that neither the social democrats nor the bolshevik faction played any significant role in it. The revolution had started without their assistance. The leading revolutionary figure of Bloody Sunday was Father George Gapon, who originally had been involved in "police socialism" and was cooperating with the social revolutionaries in initiating the revolution.

8. The "Black Hundreds" were combat groups set up by parties of the extreme right in order to fight the revolutionaries. They might be considered the ancestors of the Nazi SA and SS, though their organization was not as strong and their membership fluctuated greatly. The Black Hundreds were openly tolerated by the Tsarist police; there is, in fact, the strong possibility that the police itself secretly created these forces. The Black Hundreds rarely, if ever, succeeded in fighting the revolutionaries directly. They were used for anti-semitic pogroms, mostly in poor Jewish districts. The pogroms were lauched in the hope that counterterror ultimately would intimidate the revolutionaries. (It may be added that, according to the official version, the pogroms were "spontaneous.") This hope was based on the mistaken notion, prevalent within the Russian government and the police, that the revolutionary movement was largely the creation of Jewish international circles on whose financial and political support it depended. The assumption was that, if the Jews in Russia were made to pay for the crimes of the revolutionaries, the Jewish world leaders, in order to save their coreligionists, would call off the revolution. The frequency and violence of the pogroms have been overrated, and the utility of this anti-revolutionary tactic was very much debated within the Russian government. When it became apparent that pogroms were totally ineffective in halting the

revolution, the Black Hundreds gradually fell into disuse. Their very existence, however, provided the revolutionaries with excellent arguments for their own terror operations.

From 1906 onward, under the premiership of P. A. Stolypin, the revolutionary movement was incapacitated by systematic arrests of revolutionaries, summary executions, exiling to Siberia, and punitive expeditions against partisan bands.

9. The term "armed struggle" is another expression for "partisan action." Lenin had in mind violent actions executed by small groups for secondary objectives such as terrorism and robbery. The term does not denote armed uprising.

10. According to the official legend, the bolsheviks are opposed to terrorism. Lenin's article should dispel any false notions about the bolshevik attitude to political assassinations. Lenin makes it perfectly clear that a true bolshevik never can be against terrorism as a matter of principle: he should oppose terror only if and when murder is inexpedient and ineffective. The bolshevik, by the same token, should favor political assassinations whenever they promise to advance the communist cause.

11. Thus, Lenin admitted that many of the so-called "expropriations" were simply robberies. While Lenin did not openly advocate robberies as a convenient source of income for professional revolutionaries, the "expediency" which he championed was broad enough to include such use of "expropriations."

12. According to the Lenin Institute, Lenin was describing an expropriation which took place on 26 March 1906 at Dushet, near Tiflis, and which was carried out by six men disguised as soldiers of the 263rd Infantry Regiment. The Lenin Institute stated that 315,000 rubles were expropriated. If Lenin's party treasury received only the 200,000 rubles to which he was referring, then 115,000 rubles must have remained in the hands of the "expropriators." Souvarine commented that the robbers were socialist-federalists (that is, they belonged to one of the many splinter groups of the Social Revolutionary Party) and that the bolsheviks got hold of this money "by ruse" (*op. cit.*, p. 91). In other words, true to their Marxian philosophy, they expropriated the expropriators. Note that the action of Dushet was *not* the expropriation in which Stalin participated. Stalin earned his laurels as a bank robber on 26 June 1907 in Tiflis. In the course of that raid, no less than ten bombs were thrown and 431,000 rubles (or $170,000) seized. The Moscow expropriation was carried out on 20 March 1906 by twenty armed men who attacked a bank, disarmed four guards, and took 875,000 rubles, just as Lenin indicated in the text. For a useful discussion of some of these events, the reader is referred to Alexandre Spiridovich, *Histoire de Terrorisme Russe* (Paris: Payot, 1930).

13. *Novoye Vremya* was a leading conservative paper. During 1906, the Lettish revolutionary movement was very well organized and registered some of the more notable successes of the first Russian revolution. The Baltic provinces were the scene of a great deal of partisan action in the modern sense, which it took Russian military forces considerable time to suppress. Socialist ideology contributed only mildly to the Lettish movement's strength: nationalist feelings were a more significant fac-

tor. This is one of the first instances of the socialist-nationalist "amalgam" in guerrilla war.

14. Lenin wanted to imply that the partisan actions usually were carried out by authentic "proletarians." There is no evidence to support this statement. The "plotting intellectuals" continued to play a dominant role, and peasants were at least as important in this struggle as workers.

15. This is a reference to the Cadet party led by P. N. Milyukov.

16. While Lenin's analysis is accurate, he did underrate the importance of the national question during the first Russian revolution. Subsequently he assigned a far higher value to nationalism as a revolutionary factor.

17. Lenin was referring to the Polish Socialist party of which Joseph Pilsudski was the most prominent leader. It is significant that Pilsudski personally led one of the most daring expropriation attacks on a Polish post office himself. Lenin never participated in any of the partisan actions which he was advocating so fervently.

18. This obtuse sentence is of significance only to firm believers in the Marxian doctrine. Lenin wanted to say that some types of struggle would bring the proletariat closer to the middle classes, while others would lead it into closer relationships with the *Lumpenproletariat* and, possibly, with the very poor peasants. His point was that the socialist ideology would preserve the pure class character of the proletarian movement, regardless of the means of struggle employed by it.

19. Lenin presumably meant that if the party loses control over operations, other social forces may be able to exploit the proletarian movement for their purposes.

20. The following paragraph was written by Lenin as a footnote to his article. We have inserted it into the main text to enhance clarity.

21. Not all the bolsheviks were in favor of partisan action.

22. This amounts to Lenin *recommending* terrorism.

23. Lenin was referring to the resolution adopted by the Fourth Congress of the Russian Social Democratic Workers Party at Stockholm during April and May 1906. The difference between Lenin's views and that of the majority of the "unification congress" was considerably greater than indicated here, but Lenin at that time found it necessary to keep his peace with the party, especially since he was not certain of the wholehearted support of his bolsheviks. The Stockholm resolution opposed theft, the expropriation of private funds and of bank accounts, forced contributions, the destruction of public buildings, and railroad sabotage. Lenin succeeded in convincing the congress that it should allow the confiscation of government funds, provided expropriation could be carried out by a revolutionary organization and on its orders. The congress also approved terrorist actions in cases of self-defense.

In September 1906, the Moscow Bolshevik Party Committee issued a resolution which came out far more radically in favor of partisan war. It proclaimed "offensive tactics" to be the only useful tactics. The party was called upon to organize partisan war in cities and villages against the government. The party was to liquidate the most active representatives of the government and to seize money and arms. The resolution suggested that the population at large be invited to support the partisan war. Lenin was in favor of this more radical policy. This article in its entirety is essentially a polemic against the softer resolution of the Stockholm congress.

24. This important sentence refers to uprisings in capital cities. Many revolutionaries believed that the seizure of power could be accomplished by a sudden one-thrust insurrection against the seat of government. Lenin's remark foreshadows the development of Mao Tse-tung's operational doctrine and basically enlarges the concept of uprising into that of civil or guerrilla war.

25. This unclear sentence presumably means that it is wrong to confuse tactics with ideology. Factions of the socialist movement, distinguished from other factions largely by ideological differences, usually had a preference for specific forms of struggle. Conversely, a group specializing in one particular type of combat might be inclined to a correlated ideological orientation. Lenin suggested that the tactics of the revolutionary movement be discussed on their own merit and that ideological questions be discussed in ideological terms.

26. Commenting on Lenin's assertion that the party instead of teaching the masses is being schooled by them, and that partisan war emerged spontaneously as a riposte to actions by the Black Hundreds, the army, and the police, Souvarine said that Lenin's point could be summarized in this fashion: "All that is spontaneous is necessary." This is a paraphrase of a statement by Hegel, all too frequently quoted by Marxists: "All that is real is reasonable." Note the value which Lenin ascribed to spontaneity—a value quite at variance with the subsequent development of the "Leninist-Stalinist doctrine," which claimed to be opposed to spontaneity and placed instead the highest value on organization.

Notes to *A Viet Cong Directive on "Repression"*

1. Robert Leckie, *The Wars of America*, vol. 2 (New York, 1969).
2. Ibid.
3. William J. Miller, Henry L. Roberts, Marshall D. Shulman, *The Meaning of Communism* (Morristown, N.J., 1963).
4. "Z" was probably the code name used to designate the Security Service of Viet Cong Military Region 5.

Notes to *The Palestinian Terrorists*

1. "A leader of the Fedayeen: 'We Want a War like the Vietnam War,'" by Oriana Fallaci. *Life*, 12 June 1970.
2. Ibid.

Notes to *Terror in the United States*

1. "[Whitney] Young Says Press Builds Carmichael," *Editor & Publisher*, 20 April 1968.

2. Statistics cited in this paragraph are from *Riots, Civil and Criminal Disorders—Hearings before the Permanent Subcommittee on Investigations of the Committee on Government Operations, United States Senate*, Part 25, U.S. Government Printing Office (Washington, 1970).
3. *Radical Guide to the University of Maryland*, published by the Democratic Radical Union of Maryland (no date, but probably 1970).
4. *Hearings* (see note 2 above).

Notes to *Minimanual of the Urban Guerrilla*

1. Ernesto Guevara, "Guerra de guerrillas: un método," *Cuba Socialista*, September 1963.
2. Speech transcribed by the Latin American Monitoring Service.
4. U.S. Army Captain Charles Chandler, a veteran of the Vietnamese War, was shot and killed in October 1968 in São Paulo, Brazil, while his nine-year-old son looked on. Chandler was in the last month of a two-year study period at the University of São Paulo at the time.

   The following footnotes—in the form of "editor's notes"—were appended to the text published in *Tricontinental*:
3. Department of Public and Social Order.
5. In Brazil the expression *fazer a paquera* is used to designate the preparations for hunting paca, a mammal rodent of South American origin. By extension, the term *paquera* is used as a synonymn for checking or vigilance.

Notes to *One Hundred Fifty Questions to a Guerrilla*

1. *150 Questions for a Guerrilla*, edited by Robert K. Brown (Denver, 1963).
2. Alberto Bayo, *Mi Aporte a la Revolución Cubana* (Imp. Ejército Rebelde, Havana, 1960).

SOURCES

"Partisan Warfare," by N. Lenin. *Orbis*, a quarterly journal of world affairs published by the Foreign Policy Research Institute, Philadelphia, Pennsylvania. Translation by Regina Eldor.

Viet Cong directive on "repression." Joint United States Public Affairs Office, Saigon.

The Arafat and Khoury statements are from *Tricontinental*, Havana, Cuba.

Two articles by George Prosser. "An Introduction to Elementary Tactics": Copy provided by Senator Edward J. Gurney and the Permanent Subcommittee on Investigations.

"What Is to Be Done": *Hearings before the Permanent Subcommittee on Investigations of the Committee on Government Operations, United States Senate*, Part 25.

Minimanual of the Urban Guerrilla, by Carlos Marighella. *Tricontinental*, Havana.

150 Questions to a Guerrilla, by Alberto Bayo. Translated by Robert I. Madigan and Dr. Angel de Lumus Medina. Published by courtesy of the Air University, Montgomery, Alabama.

BIBLIOGRAPHY

Books, reports, and monographs that deal with or touch upon terrorism and
   urban guerrillas:

Andics, Hellmut. *Rule of Terror*. New York: Holt, Rinehart and Winston,
   1969.
Assassination and Political Violence, a task force of the National Commission
   on the Causes and Prevention of Violence. Washington: U.S. Govern-
   ment Printing Office, 1969.
Bain, Chester A. *Vietnam—The Roots of Conflict*. Englewood Cliffs, N.J.,
   1967.
Bennett, Richard Lawrence. *The Black and Tans*. Boston: Houghton Mifflin
   Co., 1959.
Bern, Major H. von Dach. *Total Resistance*. Boulder, Colorado: Panther
   Publications, 1965.
Black, Cyril E., and Thornton, Thomas P. *Communism and Revolution*.
   Princeton: Princeton University Press, 1964.
Bocca, Geoffrey. *The Secret Army*. Englewood Cliffs, N.J.: Prentice-Hall,
   Inc., 1968.
Browne, Malcolm W. *The New Face of War*. Indianapolis: The Bobbs-
   Merrill Co., 1965.
Clark, Michael K. *Algeria in Turmoil*. New York: Frederick A. Praeger, 1959.
Cross, James Eliot. *Conflict in the Shadows*. New York: Doubleday & Co.,
   1963.
Crozier, Brian. *South-East Asia in Turmoil*. Baltimore: Penguin Books, 1965.
Dubois, Jules. *Fidel Castro*. Indianapolis: The New Bobbs-Merrill Co., 1959.
Eckstein, Harry, ed. *Internal War*. New York: The Free Press of Glencoe,
   1964.
Giap, General Vo Nguyen. *The South Vietnam People Will Win*. Hanoi:
   Foreign Languages Publishing House, 1965.
Greene, Lt. Col. T. N., ed. *The Guerrilla—and How to Fight Him*. New
   York: Frederick A. Praeger, 1962.

Gross, Feliks. *The Seizure of Political Power in a Century of Revolutions.* New York: Philosophical Library, 1958.

Guzmán, Campos, Mons. German, Fals Borda, Orlando, and Umaña Luna, Eduardo. *La Violencia en Colombia,* vols. 1 and 2. Bogotá: Ediciones Tercer Mundo, 1963.

Hosmer, Stephen T. *Viet Cong Repression and Its Implications for the Future.* Lexington: Heath Lexington Books, 1970.

Frank, Gerold. *The Deed.* New York: Simon and Schuster, Inc., 1963.

Leiden, Carl, and Schmitt, Karl M., eds. *The Politics of Violence.* Englewood Cliffs, N.J.: Prentice Hall, Inc., 1968.

Mallin, Jay. *Terror in Viet Nam.* Princeton: D. Van Nostrand Co., 1966.

MacCarthy, J. M., ed. *Limerick's Fighting Story.* Tralee, Ireland: Anvil Books, 1966.

Marx, Karl. *Capital.* New York: International Publishers Co., 1967.

Mendel, Arthur P., ed. *Essential Works of Marxism.* New York: Bantam Books, 1965.

Mydans, Carl and Shelley. *The Violent Peace.* New York: Atheneum, 1968.

Oppenheimer, Martin. *The Urban Guerrilla.* Chicago: Quadrangle Books, 1969.

Phillips, R. Hart. *Cuba—Island of Paradox.* New York: McDowell, Obolensky, 1959.

Pike, Douglas. *The Viet-Cong Strategy of Terror.* Saigon: United States Mission, Viet-Nam, 1970.

Powers, Thomas. *Diana: The Making of a Terrorist.* Boston, 1971.

Report of the National Advisory Commission on Civil Disorders. New York: Bantam Books, 1968.

Reed, David. *111 Days in Stanleyville.* New York: Harper & Row, 1965.

Riots, Civil and Criminal Disorders—Hearings before the Permanent Subcommittee on Investigations of the Committee on Government Operations, United States Senate. Washington: U.S. Government Printing Office, 1970.

Suchlicki, Jaime. *University Students and Revolution in Cuba, 1920-1968.* Coral Gables: University of Miami Press, 1969.

Taber, Robert. *The War of the Flea.* New York: Lyle Stuart, 1965.

To Establish Justice, To Insure Domestic Tranquility. Final report of the National Commission on Causes and Prevention of Violence. New York: Bantam Books, 1970.

Trotsky, Leon. *Stalin.* New York: Harper & Brothers, 1941.

United States Mission in Viet Nam. *A Study—Viet Cong Use of Terror.* Saigon, 1967.

Whelton, Charles. *Skyjack!* New York: Tower Publications, 1970.

Wolfe, Bertram D. *Three Who Made a Revolution.* New York: The Dial Press, 1961.

INDEX

Date Due